Design and
Development Research

Design and Development Research

Methods, Strategies, and Issues

Rita C. Richey
Wayne State University

James D. Klein
Arizona State University

LEA LAWRENCE ERLBAUM ASSOCIATES, PUBLISHERS
2007 Mahwah, New Jersey   London

Director of Editorial: Lane Akers
Editorial Assistant: Anthony Messina
Cover Design: Kathryn Houghtaling-Lacey
Full-Service Compositor: MidAtlantic Books and Journals, Inc.

This book was typeset in 10.5/12 pt Goudy Old Style, Italic, Bold, and Bold Italic.
Headings were typeset in Nueva Bold Extended and Nueva Roman Bold.

Lawrence Erlbaum Associates, Inc., Publishers
10 Industrial Avenue
Mahwah, New Jersey 07430
www.erlbaum.com

**CIP information for this volume can be obtained by contacting the Library
of Congress.**

ISBN 978-0-8058-5731-3—0-8058-5731-1 (case)
ISBN 978-0-8058-5732-0—0-8058-5732-X (paper)
ISBN 978-1-4106-1692-0—1-4106-1692-4 (ebook)

Books published by Lawrence Erlbaum Associates are printed on
acid-free paper, and their bindings are chosen for strength and durability.

Printed in the United States of America

10   9   8   7   6   5   4   3   2   1

For Charlie

My partner in the best parts of life

and
Allison and Matt
Michelle and Andy

May their partnerships be as special as ours

For Jayne, Mary, and Leslie

Who make me realize the important things in life

Contents

List of Tables   xiii

List of Figures   xiv

Preface   xv

Acknowledgments   xix

1   An Overview of Design and Development Research   1

The Need for Design and Development Research   2

Design and Development as a Science   •   The Design and Development Knowledge Base and Its Foundations   •   Design and Development Research and the Advancement of the Field

The Scope of Design and Development Research   7

Research on Product and Tool Design and Development   •   Research on Design and Development Models   •   The Outcomes of Product and Tool Research and Model Research   •   The Unique Role of Design and Development Research

Looking Ahead   14

2   Identifying Design and Development Research Problems   15

Guidelines for Selecting a Research Problem   15

Sources of Design and Development Research Problems   16

*Problems from the Workplace   •   Problems Related to
Emerging Technology   •   Problems Related to Design
and Development Theory*

Using the Literature to Identify and Refine a Research Problem   25

*The Role of Literature in Problem Identification   •   Sources for
a Literature Review in Design and Development*

Focusing the Design and Development Research Problem   29

*Transforming Research Problems into Research Questions   •
Determining the Parameters of the Study*

Looking Ahead   32

A Checklist for Identifying and Focusing the Problem
of a Design and Development Study   33

3   Design and Development Research Methodology   35

The Nature of Research Design   36

*Establishing Validity   •   Facilitating Notions of Causality   •
Facilitating Generalization and Interpretation   •   Anticipating and
Avoiding Problems   •   Components of a Research Design*

The Characteristics of Design and Development
Research Methodology   39

*Commonly Used Design and Development Research Methods
and Strategies   •   Mixed and Multiple Methods Research*

Matching Research Methods and Questions   42

*Classifying Design and Development Research Goals   •
Matching Research Purposes and Methods*

Looking Ahead   45

A Checklist for Matching Design and Development Research
Questions and Methods   46

4   **Product and Tool Research: Methods and Strategies   47**

Strategies of Product Development Research   48

*A Representative Mixed Methods Case Study   •   A Representative
Multiple Qualitative Methods Study*

Strategies of Program Development Research

A Representative Program Evaluation Study

Strategies for Research on Design and Development Phases   52

*A Representative Mixed Methods Study of Formative Evaluation   •
A Representative Multiple Quantitative Methods Study
of Integrated Evaluation*

Strategies for Research on Tool Development and Use   54

*A Representative Tool Development Case Study   •   A Representative
Tool Use Study*

A Summary of Product and Tool Research Designs   57

Unique Product and Tool Research Design Concerns   61

*Researcher-Participant Dual Roles   •   Research in a Natural
Work Environment*

Looking Ahead   63

A Checklist for Addressing Common Concerns
of Product and Tool Research Design   64

5   **Model Research: Methods and Strategies   65**

Strategies of Model Development Research   66

*A Representative Multiple Qualitative Methods Study   •
A Representative Mixed Methods Study*

Strategies of Model Validation Research   67

*A Representative Expert Review Study   •   A Representative Usability
Documentation Study   •   A Representative Investigation of Component
Variables   •   A Representative Field-Evaluation Study   •
A Representative Controlled Testing Study*

Strategies of Model Use Research   72

*A Representative Expertise Study Using Think-Aloud Strategies   •
A Representative Designer Decision-Making Study Using In-Depth
Interviews   •   A Representative Qualitative Study of Conditions
Impacting Model Use*

A Summary of Model Research Designs   75

Unique Model Research Design Concerns   78

*Working with Recall Data   •   Research in Multiple Natural Work
Environments   •   Distinguishing Participant Characteristics*

Looking Ahead   81

A Checklist for Addressing Common Concerns
of Model Research Design   82

6   **Selecting Participants and Settings   83**

Selecting the Setting of the Study   84

*Types of Settings and Their Characteristics   •   Matching Settings
to Research Questions   •   Practical Issues in Setting Selection*

Selecting the Participants of the Study   87

Types of Participants   •   Sampling Participants

Participant and Setting Solutions from the Design
and Development Literature   90

*Participants and Settings in Product and Tool Research   •
Participants and Settings in Model Research*

Ethical Consideration for the Protection of Participants   94

*Getting Approval to Conduct Research   •   Obtaining Informed
Consent   •   Avoiding Coercion   •   Maintaining Confidentiality
and Ensuring Anonymity*

Looking Ahead   96

A Checklist for Selecting Participants and Settings
in a Design and Development Study   97

7   Collecting Design and Development Research Data   99

    Critical Design and Development Research Data   100

      *Profile Data   •   Context Data   •   In-Progress Project Data   •
Try-Out Data*

    Data Collection Instruments   106

      *Work Logs   •   Surveys and Questionnaires   •   Interview
Protocols   •   Observation Guides*

    Technology-Based Data Collection Strategies   117

      *Web-Based Data Collection   •   Software-Based Data
Collection   •   Laboratory-Based Data Collection*

    Data Collection Issues   123

      Ensuring Data Integrity   •   Establishing Appropriate Data Sets

    Looking Ahead   125

    A Checklist for Collecting Data in a Design
and Development Study   126

8   Interpreting Design and Development Findings   127

    The Contributions of Design and Development Research   127

      *Expanding the Design and Development Knowledge Base   •
Creating the Foundations for Design and Development Theory   •
Creating the Foundations for Future Research*

    Interpreting Product and Tool Research Findings   132

      *Lessons Learned about Product and Tool Design and Development
Processes   •   Lessons Learned about Product and Tool Use*

    Interpreting Model Research Findings   135

      *Understanding Model Development Findings   •   Understanding Model
Validation Findings   •   Understanding Model Use Findings*

    Interpretation Issues   139

      *Generalizations and Project-Specific Data   •   The Impact
of Organizational Concerns*

Looking Ahead   142

A Checklist for Interpreting Findings of Design
and Development Research   143

9   **The Status and Future of Design and Development Research   145**

The Expansion of Design and Development Research   146

Alternative Approaches to Design and Development Research   •
New Opportunities for Design and Development Research

Conditions that Facilitate Design and Development Research   151

Dissatisfaction with Existing Research Orientations   •   Knowledge of the
Innovation   •   Availability of Resources

Conclusions   153

Glossary of Terms   155
References   161
Author Index   173
Subject Index   177

Tables

1–1   Representative Clusters of Design and Development Research
1–2   The Varying Outcomes of Design and Development Research
2–1   Journals Relating to Design and Development Research
3–1   Common Methods Employed in Design and Development Research
3–2   Representative Matches between Purposes, Methods and Types of Design and Development Research
4–1   Representative Research Design Techniques Used in Product and Tool Research
5–1   Representative Research Design Techniques Used in Model Research
6–1   Settings of Design and Development Applications
6–2   Setting Elements that Impact Design and Development Research
6–3   Common Participants in Design and Development Studies
7–1   Critical Profile Data in Design and Development Research
7–2   Critical Context Data in Design and Development Research
7–3   Critical In-Progress Data in Design and Development Research
7–4   Critical Try-Out Data in Design and Development Research
7–5   Design and Development Data Accessible via Technology
7–6   Sample Hardware and Software Specifications for a Basic Design and Development Research Laboratory
8–1   Product and Tool Design and Development Process Conclusions and Supporting Data
8–2   Product and Tool Use Conclusions and Supporting Data
8–3   Model Development Conclusions and Supporting Data
8–4   Model Validation Conclusions and Supporting Data
8–5   Model Use Conclusions and Supporting Data

Figures

1–1   The IDD Knowledge Base

1–2   The Research and Theory Foundations of the Design and Development Knowledge Base

2–1   Narrowing the Research Topic

7–1   An Overview of Data Collection Tools Used in McKenney (2002)

7–2   Basic Designer/Developer Work Log for In-Progress Projects

7–3   Task-Oriented Designer/Developer Work Log for Past Projects

7–4   Sample Designer Characteristic Survey

7–5   Sample Product Evaluation Survey

7–6   Sample Designer Interview Questions

7–7   A Critical Incident Interview Protocol With Probes

7–8   Sample Classroom Observation Checklist from Ottevanger (2000)

7–9   Sample Open-Ended Observation Instrument

8–1   Expanding the Designer and Design Processes Knowledge Base Through Design and Development Research Findings

Preface

This book is intended for scholars who are interested in planning and conducting design and development research. It is written for experienced researchers, as well as those who are preparing to become researchers. We made two main assumptions about our audience while writing this book. First, you should be familiar with concepts and principles related to research design and methods. The book is intended to supplement a standard research methods text, not replace it. Second, you should have knowledge related to processes and models of design and development.

THE EVOLUTION OF DESIGN
AND DEVELOPMENT RESEARCH

Many examples of design and development research can be found in the literature spanning up to four decades. In recent years, however, there has been renewed interest in this research orientation and the benefits it offers the field. Furthermore, notions of design and development research continue to evolve. We are defining design and development research here as

> the systematic study of design, development and evaluation processes with the aim of establishing an empirical basis for the creation of instructional and non-instructional products and tools and new or enhanced models that govern their development.

Our current thinking about this type of research has changed in two ways. Readers familiar with our earlier work will note the use of the term "design and development research" in this book. Previously, we used the term "developmental research" to describe this approach (Richey, Klein, & Nelson, 2004; Richey & Klein, 2005; Richey & Nelson, 1996; Seels & Richey, 1994). Discussions with colleagues and students suggest, however, that the word "developmental" creates confusion since it refers to many other areas of study, such as human development, international development, organizational development, and staff development.

Furthermore, over the years, the term "development" has been ambiguous to many in the field and has generated considerable discussion regarding its meaning. This debate has focused typically upon the distinctions between instructional design and instructional development. In defining the domains of the field, Seels and Richey (1994) viewed design as the planning phase in which specifications are constructed, and development as the production phase in which the design specifications are actualized. Others broadly define each of the terms so that they have similar meanings. For example, Briggs (1977) defined *instructional design* as "the entire process of analysis of learning needs and goals and the development of a delivery system to meet the needs; includes development of instructional materials and activities; and tryout and revision of all instruction and learner assessment activities." In this interpretation, design is the more generic term, encompassing *both* planning and production. In contrast, Smaldino, Russell, Heinich, and Molenda (2005) define *instructional development* as "the process of analyzing needs, determining what content must be mastered, establishing educational goals, designing materials to reach the objectives, and trying out and revising the program in terms of learner achievement" (p. 386). To many in the field, this is a definition of the instructional systems design (ISD) process.

We purposely use the term *design* and *development* throughout this book because together they have a broad meaning especially in the research context. The focus of a design and development study can be on front-end analysis, planning, production, and/or evaluation. This approach can also center on the design and development of products and tools or on the development, validation and use of design and development models. In essence, this is the *study* of design and development processes as opposed to performing them.

Another change in our thinking relates to the field's traditional emphasis on instructional interventions. While many of the examples of design and development research do focus on *instructional* products, tools and models, our definition includes the study of both instructional and non-instructional interventions. This is in keeping with expanded definitions of the field that encompass notions of performance improvement and non-instructional interventions (Reiser, 2002).

OVERVIEW OF THE BOOK

Throughout this book, we have included an explanation of the methods and strategies appropriate for design and development research. We also discuss issues and problems that design and development researchers often confront when planning and conducting a study. Procedural explanations are supported by a wide variety of examples of research studies from the literature and by samples of actual research tools. We provide checklists to assist you in planning and conducting each phase of a design and development study. An extensive reference list and a glossary of terms are also included. Below we describe the nine chapters that make up the main body of the book.

Chapter 1, "An Overview of Design and Development Research," examines why this type of research is important to advance the knowledge base of the field and offers a rationale for further studies of this type. The scope of design and development research is examined, and its two categories—product and tool studies and model studies—are defined.

Chapter 2, "Identifying Design and Development Research Problems," provides practical guidelines for how to select and evaluate a research topic and problem to study. Sources of design and development research problems are discussed, including the workplace, emerging technology, and theory. Several sources of design and development literature are also provided. The chapter closes with an explanation of how to transform a research problem into a question and establish the parameters of a design and development study.

Chapter 3, "Design and Development Research Methodology," explores the nature of research design and describes some general concerns that should be addressed in any research project. Concerns such as validity, generalizability, and causality are discussed. The methods and strategies commonly employed in design and development research studies are described. Suggestions for how to match research questions to methods are also provided.

Chapter 4, "Product and Tool Research: Methods and Strategies," examines the research design strategies used in representative studies of this type. Several in-depth examples are provided to illustrate how to plan research studies related to product and program development, the various phases of design and development, and the development and use of tools. The chapter ends with a discussion of two issues that should be addressed when conducting product and tool research: (a) avoiding bias when researchers assume participant roles and (b) recognizing the influence of work environment characteristics.

Chapter 5, "Model Research: Methods and Strategies," focuses on the design of studies of the development, validation, and use of design and development models. Numerous detailed examples are used to show how to plan and conduct this type of design and development research. Issues such as working with recall data, conducting research in multiple natural work settings, and distinguishing participant characteristics are discussed.

Chapter 6, "Selecting Participants and Settings," explores issues related to who will participate in the design and development research project and where the study will be conducted. Several examples of participants and settings that have been examined in actual design and development studies, and brief

analyses of techniques that have been employed are provided. Ethical considerations for the protection of participants such as obtaining informed consent, avoiding coercion, and maintaining confidentiality and anonymity are
also discussed.

Chapter 7, "Collecting Data in Design and Development Research," examines the critical types of information that are often gathered in a design
and development study. These include profile data, context data, in-progress
project data, and try-out data. Commonly used data collection tools such as
work logs, surveys, questionnaires, interview protocols, and observation guides
are described, as is the use of technology for data collection. Sample instruments are provided. In addition, issues related to ensuring data integrity are
discussed.

Chapter 8, "Interpreting Design and Development Findings," examines how
results from these studies can be used to expand the knowledge base and create a foundation for theory and future research. The major types of conclusions
that can be made by design and development researchers, as well as the key
types of data that are used to support these conclusions, are discussed.

Chapter 9, "The Status and Future of Design and Development Research,"
explores the manner in which design and development research is expanding,
as well as the conditions that facilitate such growth. This chapter includes a
description of design-based research and formative research, two alternative
approaches that can be used to address problems similar to those dealt with
by design and development researchers. Finally, we speculate on the future
design and development research pertaining to technology, workplace issues
and theory.

This is a book of methods, strategies and issues related to design and development research. We have tried to provide concrete direction for those em-
barking on such projects, as well as stimulate future thinking about this type of
endeavor. Hopefully, this book will increase your understanding of design and
development research, and motivate you to tackle such a project yourself.

Rita C. Richey   James D. Klein
Detroit, Michigan   Tempe, Arizona

Acknowledgments

We want to recognize the many people who have supported us in this project and in the advancement of design and development research. Bob Reiser has been a great proponent of this research for many years. His public advocacy and private encouragement have meant a great deal to both of us. He has carried on the support Barb Seels and Walt Dick gave to this topic in the early years of our work. Monica Tracey became an adherent of design and development research first as a doctoral student, and now as a faculty member. She regularly spreads the word and has served us especially in terms of her feedback and reviews of this manuscript. Likewise, Kathryn Ley has enthusiastically promoted this research through conference presentations and repeated calls of "So when's the book going to be done?" Finally, Susan McKenney has been a great help to the preparation of this book. She has shared much of her own work with us and provided insights into her experiences with design and development research.

Some of the best assessments of this book throughout its development have come from the students at Wayne State University and Arizona State University. They have read chapters (often not by choice), critiqued them, and told us what helps and what doesn't, always with great clarity.

There has also been a level of support from the Erlbaum group that we greatly appreciate. Both Lori Kelly and Lane Akers have been behind this project from the beginning. They have secured wonderful reviewers who provided direction for us throughout the writing process, and Lane has been particularly helpful as we reach the end of the journey.

Finally, we want to acknowledge Bill Winn's contributions to the research in this field. We hope that this book will help advance the high standards that he set for us.

1

An Overview
of Design and
Development Research

This book is about how to plan and conduct design and development research. These methods are also known as developmental or development research (Richey, Klein, & Nelson, 2004; Seels & Richey, 1994; van den Akker, 1999). Design and development research seeks to create knowledge grounded in data systematically derived from practice. We define this type of research as:

> the systematic study of design, development and evaluation processes with the aim of establishing an empirical basis for the creation of instructional and non-instructional products and tools and new or enhanced models that govern their development.

This is a pragmatic type of research that offers a way to test theory and to validate practice that has been perpetuated essentially through unchallenged tradition. In addition, it is a way to establish new procedures, techniques, and tools based upon a methodical analysis of specific cases.

The design and development of instructional products and programs is considered by many to be the heart of the instructional design and technology (IDT) field. Practitioners in the field typically follow well-established systematic models and procedures to design and develop instructional and non-instructional interventions. These approaches are advocated (and have been used) in a wide range of education and training environments. They include a set of common characteristics, including a focus on measurable goals and outcomes derived through an initial analysis phase, the selection of content and strategies that match these goals, a process of routinely evaluating the products prior to finalizing the project, and the assessment of the learning and performance outcomes (Gustafson & Branch, 2002; Seels & Glasgow, 1998).[1]

The practice of design and development is to a great extent empirical by nature. Design models parallel the scientific problem-solving processes. It would not be unreasonable, then, to assume that design and development processes themselves would have robust empirical support. However, historically there has been a paucity of research on our models, tools, and products.

THE NEED FOR DESIGN AND DEVELOPMENT RESEARCH

Over the last five decades, many scholars have called for research to strengthen the fundamental knowledge base of the IDT field. In 1953, Finn asserted that the audio-visual field suffered from a dominance of "gadgeteering" that reflected a "poverty of thought" (p. 13) and suggested that research would help professionalize the field. A decade later, Markle (1967) called for the development of empirically grounded instructional materials through systematic testing procedures. In 1984, Heinich stressed the importance of field-based research to inform practice. More recently, Richey (1997) suggested that "our practice is not sufficiently informed by research and that our research is not sufficiently attuned to practice" (p. 91).

Design and Development as a Science

Opinions on the role of research on design and development often depend on one's conception of what it actually is. We take the position that design and development is a science. As a science it should be bound by understandings built upon replicated empirical research. Our models and procedures should be validated. The solutions to our problems should be supported by data. This, however, is not a universally accepted position.

---

[1]Readers who are not familiar with instructional design and development should consult some of the standard references to gain further knowledge of the field. These books include *The Systematic Design of Instruction* by Dick, Carey, and Carey (2005), *Designing Effective Instruction* by Morrison, Ross, and Kemp, (2006), and *Instructional Design* by Smith and Ragan, (2005).

Davies (1981) first presented the question of whether this field was an art, a craft or a science, opting for the artistic orientation. He viewed design and development as a holistic process, one that cannot be simply analyzed and dissected. It is a view that emphasizes the systemic over the systematic.

Others have also explored the essential nature of the field. For example, Visscher-Voerman and Gustafson's (2004) study of practicing instructional designers shows that some designers follow an instrumental design paradigm that is rooted in the natural sciences. This approach is akin to the traditional instructional systems design model (ISD). Others employ an artistic paradigm. This approach is one that eschews scientific methods and "dissolves the borders between the domains of the sciences and the arts" (p. 83).

Clark and Estes (1998) view many of the solutions to educational problems as craft. They define craft as skills that are based upon "fortunate accidents, personal experience, insights . . . revised through trial and error" (p. 6). As an alternative, they advocate following a technology orientation in which problems are addressed through the use of scientific theory.

Like Clark and Estes, we approach design and development (and, in turn, research on it) with the assumption that science and empiricism provide a more effective and reliable route to disciplinary integrity than depending on artistic tactics and craft-based solutions. We believe that our field has not sufficiently employed scientific methods to facilitate our understanding of design and development processes. The need for research is especially critical with respect to the models and processes employed by designers and developers. Few models, design strategies, and tools employed in practice have been empirically tested and validated. This is the gap that design and development research seeks to address.

The Design and Development Knowledge Base and Its Foundations

The field, of course, is not devoid of research. A large and comprehensive base of knowledge informs our work. From our perspective, the design and development knowledge base has six major components. These six facets focus on the different elements of the design and development enterprise: (a) learners and how they learn, (b) the context in which learning and performance occur, (c) the nature of content and how it is sequenced, (d) the instructional strategies and activities employed, (e) the media and delivery systems used, and lastly, (f) the designers themselves and the processes they use. Figure 1–1 portrays the overlapping elements of this knowledge base.

This knowledge base has been shaped over the years by a combination of the foundational research and theory of other disciplines as well as the research and theory unique to instructional design and development. There are three

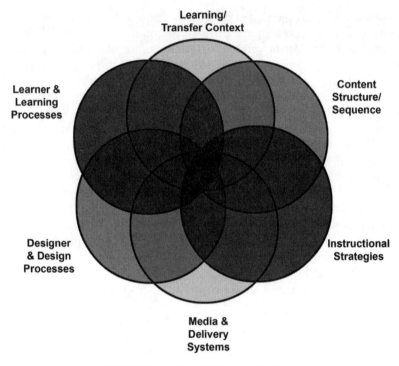

FIGURE 1–1.   The IDD knowledge base.

key lines of research and theory that have had the most influence on the design and development knowledge base. These are

- Psychological and learning theory and research.
- Instructional theory and teaching-learning research.
- Communication theory and message design research.

Psychological and learning theory and research provides the dominant foundations for knowledge and practice pertaining to: (a) the learner and the learning process, (b) the learning and transfer context, and (c) instructional strategies. Instructional design (ID) is intimately tied to human learning and today is being extended to organizational learning. Originally, behavioral explanations of the learning process were dominant in instructional design. While there is still some evidence of behavioral thinking, cognitive principles are often followed when devising strategies that facilitate motivation for learning, as well as the understanding, retention, and use of learned information. And today, there is a great deal of interest in the view that "(1) learning is an active process of constructing rather than acquiring knowledge and (2) instruction is a process of supporting that construction rather than communication of knowledge" (Duffy & Cunningham, 1996, p. 171). In this orientation emphasis is placed upon the social context of learning, collaboration, and learner control.

Next, instructional theory and teaching-learning research provides the foundations for knowledge and practice pertaining to (a) content structure and sequence, (b) instructional strategies, and (c) media and delivery systems. While instructional theory is necessarily prescriptive in nature, it is typically intertwined with the orientation of a particular learning theory.

Most strategies for presenting instruction are rooted in instructional theory (Reigeluth, 1983; Richey, 1986). One example of a theory of instruction is Gagne's (1985) Events of Instruction. This theory suggests a particular sequence of instructional activities that can be incorporated into a lesson to facilitate learning and transfer. Constructivist orientations to learning, which avoid the "presentation" of content in favor of students controlling their own learning activities, also rely upon instructional theories and teaching-learning research.

The vast majority of design and development approaches assume that instruction should vary depending upon the type of learning task being addressed. Another important design decision, the selection of media and delivery systems, is typically guided by instructional principles, such as those relating to facilitating learner involvement in "real-world" activities. Currently, the growing use of distance education methodologies is stimulating teaching-learning research in this area, and this work should be of increasing importance to designers and developers.

Lastly, communications theory and message design research has provided the major foundations for knowledge and practice pertaining to media and delivery systems. When combined with the principles of information processing and perception, communication theory tenets and message-design principles guide page layout, screen design, graphics, and visual design. Research relevant to gaining and controlling attention has been of particular importance to the design and development field.

Traditionally, this type of research and theory has been crucial to all media design. Today, its major impact is on the development of interactive, computer-based media and Web design. In all cases, however, this type of research is fundamental to the study and applications of visual thinking, visual learning, and visual communication.

While psychological research, teaching-learning research and message-design research all have implications for design and development, this body of literature does not fully address the last component of the IDD knowledge base: the designer and design processes. It does not explain, for example, the role of the designer or the context in which design and development takes place. It does not explain designer problem-solving processes. It does not speak to the ultimate value of ID models, or of ways of reducing design cycle time, or of the most effective and efficient ways of using learning objects when designing instruction using advanced technologies. Design and development research is the primary source of such knowledge, but, unfortunately, there is only a limited amount of this type of research. Our position is that this shortage ultimately impedes not only design and development practice, but scholarship in the field as well.

Design and Development Research and the Advancement of the Field

Instructional design, and hence its practice, can be seen in two ways: (a) the design of particular lessons, products, or programs, and (b) the implementation and management of the overall design process. The former is guided by design principles for selecting and sequencing instructional strategies that are richly supported by learning theory and teaching-learning research (Ragan & Smith, 2004). The latter is typically guided by instructional system design (ISD) models which have not been tested to a great extent using research. Historically, ISD models were devised as an application of General Systems Theory (Banathy, 1968), but systems theory derived its support from deductive logic rather than empirical research. This pattern continues today with respect not only to new design and development models, but also for newly devised approaches to producing instruction and other interventions utilizing advanced technologies. This meager research base, in turn, makes it impossible for scholars to construct sound and comprehensive design and development theory.

We posit that design and development research will not only enhance our knowledge base, but will also provide the empirical basis for the construction of a comprehensive theory of design and development. This will give the field a fourth theory base, supplementing the understandings we have already acquired from psychological and learning theory, instructional and teaching-learning theory, and communication and message-design theory. The research and theory foundations of the design and development knowledge base would then be as shown in Figure 1–2.

This research and theory is as vital to the advancement of design and development practice as it is to the scholarly advancement of the field.

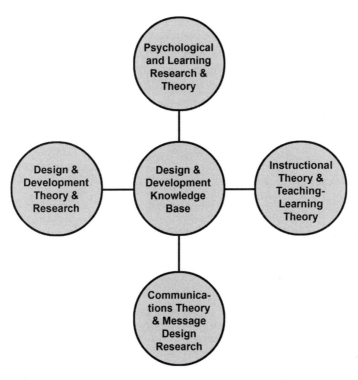

FIGURE 1–2. The research and theory foundations of the design and development knowledge base.

THE SCOPE OF DESIGN
AND DEVELOPMENT RESEARCH

Design and development research covers a wide spectrum of activities and interests. In its simplest form, it could be either

- The study of the process and impact of specific design and development efforts.
- The study of the design and development process as a whole, or of particular process components.

Such research can involve a situation in which someone is studying the design and development work of others. However, it can also involve a situation in which someone is performing design and development activities and studying the process at the same time. In either case, there is a distinction between *doing* design and development and *studying* the processes.

Understanding the nature of this research is a matter of understanding the range of problems to which it can be applied. It is also a process of recognizing those research interests and endeavors that are *not* a part of this orientation. Design and development research, as with all research endeavors, leads to knowledge production, a more complete understanding of the field, and the ability to make predictions. Design and development research accomplishes these goals through two large categories of research projects:

- Product and tool research.
- Model research.

Understanding these categories can facilitate an appreciation of the breadth and depth of design and development research.

Within each of these two major types of design and development research various lines of inquiry have emerged over the years. Table 1–1 shows many of these lines of study.

Clearly these research clusters are not all that exist or that could fit within the two major divisions of design and development research. They do, how-

TABLE 1–1.
Representative Clusters of Design and Development Research

Design & Development Research	
Product & Tool Research	*Model Research*
Comprehensive Design and Development Projects • Instructional Products & Programs • Non-instruction Products & Programs	Model Development • Comprehensive Model Development • Development of Model Component Processes
Specific Project Phases • Analysis • Design • Development • Evaluation	Model Validation • Internal Validation of Model Components • External Validation of Model Impact
Design & Development Tools • Tool Development • Tool Use	Model Use • Study of Conditions Impacting Model Use • Designer Decision-Making Research • Designer Expertise & Characteristics Research

ever, show the broad scope of research that is encompassed within the domain of design and development research. We will now summarize the kinds of studies that fit within the two types of design and development research—product and tool research and model research.

Research on Product and Tool Design and Development

The most straightforward design and development research falls into the first category: research conducted during the design and development of a product or tool. Often the entire design and development process is documented. Some research, however, concentrates on one aspect of design and development only (such as production) or de-emphasizes some phases (such as needs assessment). Many recent studies focus on the design and development of technology-based instruction. In this research there is a tendency to combine the task of doing design and development and studying the processes.

Product and tool research typically involves situations in which the design and development process used in a particular situation is described, analyzed, and a final product is evaluated. Driscoll (1984) used the term "systems-based evaluation" to describe a similar research paradigm, while van den Akker (1999) labeled it as "formative research." van den Akker further defines this as "research activities performed during the entire development process of a specific intervention, from exploratory studies through (formative and summative) evaluation studies" (p. 6). We previously referred to this category of design and development research as Type 1 developmental studies (Richey, Klein, & Nelson, 2004).

Product development research. Product studies originate with the design and development of an instructional or non-instructional product or program. They demonstrate a range of design and development principles available to practitioners. Frequently, the entire design and development process is documented. Consistent with predominant practice in the field, the procedures employed usually follow the tenets of ISD, encompassing front-end analysis through evaluation. For example, Hirumi, Savenye, and Allen (1994) describe the analysis, design, and development of an interactive videodisc exhibit in a natural history museum. Furthermore, a field evaluation was conducted to examine visitors' use of the videodisc by focusing on "the program's ability to attract and hold viewers' attention, and visitors' interaction with the program" (p. 51). This study provides evidence that ISD processes can be adapted to informal educational settings.

Other studies emphasize a particular design and development phase, such as needs assessment or evaluation. For example, Klein et al. (2000) report on a needs assessment conducted to determine the optimal instructional content and delivery method for an introductory course in educational technology. The results of the needs assessment were used to revise an existing course. Fischer, Savenye, and Sullivan (2002) report on the evaluation of a computer-based training course for an online financial and purchasing system. The purpose of the study was to evaluate the effectiveness of the training and to identify appropriate revisions to incorporate into the program.

Tool development research. Instructional designers use a variety of tools in the course of a project. These tools range from paper-based job aids to electronic performance support systems (EPSS). In recent years there has been an effort to develop computer-based tools intended to automate many design and development processes. These include tools for identifying and structuring content, for selecting strategies for learners, and for authoring instructional programs (Li & Merrill, 1991; Merrill & Li, 1989). Design and development research can focus on the development and the efficacy of these tools.

For example, Nieveen and van den Akker (1999) reported on the development and evaluation of five prototypes of a computer system to support designers during formative evaluation. This study exemplifies tool development research; it includes a careful and extensive documentation of the phases of ISD—needs analysis, design, development, and formative evaluation of several prototypes of a performance support tool. Another example of a tool study is Preese and Foshay's (1999) research on the development, quality assurance, and impact of a set of object-oriented authoring tools. This study has not only project-specific conclusions, but it also identifies lessons that can apply to other large-scale CBT development projects. These two studies show how research techniques have been employed to study the development and validation of tools for instructional designers.

Recent research has also focused on non-instructional tools. For example, Nguyen (2005) described a needs assessment conducted to determine the types of EPSS that training professionals and end users think are valuable to facilitate performance. In addition, Nguyen, Klein, and Sullivan (2005) conducted an experiment in which employees at a manufacturing company completed a procedural task and received support from either an intrinsic, extrinsic, or external EPSS or received no support. The authors suggest how to improve user performance by integrating support with work tasks. Thus, conclusions are aimed at designers.

Research on Design and Development Models

The second type of design and development research pertains to studies of the development, validation, and use of design and development models.

These studies focus on the models and processes themselves, rather than their demonstration. While it is possible to conduct model research in conjunction with the development of a product or program, most model studies concentrate on previously developed instruction, and consequently are not project-specific. Model research may address the validity or effectiveness of an existing or newly constructed development model, process, or technique. In addition, these studies often seek to identify and describe the conditions that facilitate successful design and development.

Model research is the most generalized of design and development research. The ultimate object of this research is the production of new knowledge, often in the form of a new (or an enhanced) design or development model. This research may emphasize comprehensive models or particular design techniques or processes. It commonly examines design and development as it is practiced in the workplace. In this section, we will describe a number of studies to clarify the nature of model research.

Model development research. One genre of design and development research results in the development of new or enhanced models to guide the ID process. For example, Spector, Muraida, and Marlino (1992) proposed an enhanced ISD model for use in courseware authoring, which is grounded in cognitive theory. This use of the model was then described and evaluated in a military training environment. Another example is Carliner's (1998) naturalistic study of design practices in a museum setting in which an enhanced model of instructional design for informal learning in museums was proposed as an outcome of the research. Finally, Plass and Salisbury (2002) described and evaluated a design model for a Web-based knowledge management system. This model includes not only the initial development of the knowledge management system, but provides for further development and maintenance to accommodate changing needs.

The newly developed models, however, need not relate to the entire design and development process. Some studies focus only on a part of the process. For example, Forsyth (1998) addressed only the development of a train-the-trainer model and she concentrated on one particular setting, non-profit community-based training environments. Her data describes the specific steps completed when following her model, the time allocated to each phase of the model and the lessons learned throughout.

Model validation research. Model construction, however, is only one of the researchable issues that can be addressed with a design and development study. Today, many recognize that ID models should be substantiated by systematic validation rather than relying primarily on user testimonials as evidence of their effectiveness (Gustafson & Branch, 2002). ID model validation is an empirical process that demonstrates the effectiveness of a model's use in the workplace or provides support for the various components of the model itself (Richey, 2005). This is an important type of design and development research.

Often model validation efforts are combined with model development research. One such example is that of Sleezer (1991) who developed and validated a Performance Analysis for Training (PAT) Model using expert review methods. She used experts in training needs assessment to evaluate the content and face validity of the PAT model. This is an example of an internal validation study, a validation of the components and processes of an ID model. Studies such as these focus upon the integrity of the model and its use.

There are also external validation studies that confirm the model not by verifying its components, but by documenting the impact of the model's use. These studies address the instructional products produced by following the model, and the impact of these products on learners, clients, and organizations. In many respects, these studies can be seen as summative or confirmative evaluations of the model. For example, a few studies have validated the ARCS Model of Motivational Design (Keller, 1987) by studying the impact of the various model components (e.g., attention, relevance, confidence, and satisfaction) on achievement (Brolin, Milheim, & Viechnicki, 1993–94; Means, Jonassen, & Dwyer, 1997; Small & Gluck, 1994).

Model use research. It is not unusual for model validation studies to address usability issues; however, there is another group of design and development studies that address these processes by *concentrating* on their use. These studies may focus on the conditions that affect model use in an effort to identify the impact of the various design and development environments. Other model use studies focus on the designers themselves in an effort to understand the design and development process as it is actually performed.

Several studies can serve as examples of these model use foci. Roytek (2000) conducted an extensive examination of two design projects that employed rapid prototyping procedures in an effort to determine which contextual factors influence project success. The instructional support factor was most closely related to the work of the designers and developers. In another study, Spector, Muraido, and Marlino (1992) examined the variables that affect the ability of designers to effectively author computer-based instruction.

Rowland's (1992) comprehensive study of the use of design models serves as an example of both designer decision-making research and research on designer characteristics. Four expert and four novice designers were given a task to design instruction for an industrial setting involving training employees to operate two hypothetical machines. The thoughts designers had while completing the task were coded and analyzed. The results of this study describe how design processes actually work and compare the differences between how experts and novices design instruction.

The Outcomes of Product and Tool Research and Model Research

In the contemporary orientation toward research, most accept the premise that research can have a broader function than the creation of generalizable statements of law; context-specific studies also are valued. Design and development research encompasses studies with conclusions that are both generalizable and contextually specific. This reflects the fact that product and tool research typically involves studies that describe and analyze the design and development processes used in *particular* projects, and are thus to a great extent context-bound. Model research studies, on the other hand, are oriented toward a general analysis of design and development processes. These studies tend to be more generalizable than product studies. Table 1–2 portrays the relationships between the two major types of design and development research.

All of these studies, however, can provide some direction to others in the field, even those whose conclusions are derived from particular projects and contexts. The "lessons learned" from these studies can apply to those who are confronting similar design and development projects. Model studies may generate new or enhanced models available for general use, but not all have such a comprehensive goal. They may explain the way in which existing models are used; they may account for success and failures of model use.

TABLE 1–2.
The Varying Outcomes of Design
and Development Research

	Design & Development Research	
	Product & Tool Research	*Model Research*
Emphasis	Study of specific product or tool design and development projects	Study of model development, validation or use
Outcome	Lessons learned from developing specific products and analyzing the conditions which facilitate their use	New design and development procedures or models, and conditions which facilitate their use

Context-Specific
Conclusions $\Rightarrow$ $\Rightarrow$ $\Rightarrow$ $\Rightarrow$ Generalized
Conclusions

The Unique Role of Design and Development Research

Design and development research—both product and tool research and model research—covers a broad array of design and development issues. It spans all phases of the design and development process, the various education and training settings in which designers work, and encompasses all design philosophies and orientations. Unlike most other research efforts, design and development research is in a position to substantially expand the theory base of ID by reaching beyond the traditional foundations of teaching and learning research. Design and development researchers are also in a position to directly impact the work of practitioners, especially because of the propensity of these researchers to situate their studies in natural work settings and to address the pressing problems of the workplace. These researchers value the importance of learning and performance, but also view the designer as a key element in the design and development process. In many respects, design and development research serves as an important link between theory and practice.

LOOKING AHEAD

We have provided an overview of design and development research in this chapter. We indicated *why* this type of research is important and offered a rationale for further studies of this type. We also focused on *what* design and development research is by defining its scope and its categories, but we have not yet discussed *how* to conduct design and development research. In the next chapter, we will begin to tackle these procedures by focusing on how to identify a research problem for a design and development study. We will examine the sources, characteristics, and parameters of problems that relate to conducting design and development research.

2

Identifying Design and Development Research Problems

Several years ago, one of us attended the first meeting of a "research interest group" where many of the participants (who were doctoral students in instructional systems) introduced themselves by saying, "I'm just starting my research project and trying to figure out my problem." After several such introductions, it became clear that while most of the world was seeking answers, we were seeking questions.

Identifying a research problem and related questions is the first step in planning any empirical study. This can be difficult, especially for those who are planning their first study or for those searching for a new research agenda. This difficulty is further compounded by the search for *important* problems and questions. Research problems in design and development should address important questions that contribute to our knowledge base and to the improvement of our practice.

GUIDELINES FOR SELECTING A RESEARCH PROBLEM

Other authors suggest some practical guidelines for identifying a research problem. Patten (2002), for example, recommends that novice researchers should start by identifying a few broad problem areas of interest (such as distance education, performance analysis, or rapid prototyping) and then evaluate each area by asking, "Is the problem area in the mainstream of the field?" "Is there a substantial body of literature in the area?" "Is the problem timely?" Gall, Gall, and Borg (2003) advise that research problems should be based on factors such as (a) significance (Is it important?), (b) feasibility (Do you have the resources and expertise necessary to study it?) and (c) benefit (Is it directly related to your professional goals?). Tuckman (1999) indicates that a good research problem is clearly and unambiguously stated in question form; is testable by empirical, data-based methods; and does not represent a moral or ethical position.

The value, authenticity, and the perceived relevance of a design and development research project depend to a great extent upon the problem selected. Thus, the search for research problems is indeed a critical part of the research effort. This search begins with converting a *topic* of interest into a researchable *problem* worth addressing. Topics are relatively easy to identify; problem identification is more complex.

Some problems are more worthy of your time and energy than others. Good problems are of interest not only to the researcher, but also to the profession at large. Good problems for a particular researcher are those to which he or she brings existing knowledge, skill, and experience. Good problems are those that can be solved in the time available.

The nature of a research problem not only predicts interest in the project, but also whether the study is viewed as relevant. According to Richey (1998), "explorations of research relevance are typically examinations of shared perceptions, the extent to which researchers' notions of relevance are congruent with the perceptions and needs of practitioners" (p. 8). This is particularly true with research on design and development where the object of such research is not simply knowledge, but knowledge that practitioners can use.

SOURCES OF DESIGN AND DEVELOPMENT
RESEARCH PROBLEMS

Where do you find really important research problems? This is the dilemma of all researchers. While the particular interests of individual researchers guide much research, there are other sources of research problems. Three areas that are ready sources of design and development research problems are:

- Actual workplace settings and projects.
- Technology (especially the newer and more innovative examples).
- The most traditional stimulus to new research—theoretical questions prompted by current research and development literature.

Problems from the Workplace

For those involved in design and development research, the problems are often found by listening to practitioners. The workplace is a primary source of research problems. An astute researcher can identify many problems and questions by observing how design and development is done in a particular setting, by discussing ID practices with designers, or by reflecting on his or her own practice. Not only are the experiences and concerns of those in various workplace settings important stimuli to this type of research, but actual projects themselves can also serve as the focus of design and development research. Thus, the research is rooted in the objectives and the complexities of practice. The problems are explicitly defined and the solutions are interpreted in light of the workplace's contextual details.

Characteristics of workplace problems. What are the problems that are found routinely on the job? Certainly, there are many. However, to be *noticed* as a researchable workplace problem and to be considered critical, a situation typically needs to be:

- Recurring and common to many settings.
- Viewed as basically solvable.
- Reflective of broad areas of current interest in the field.

There are some job-related issues that seem to be more or less permanently embedded in the field, such as how to simultaneously reduce development time and costs, or how to get knowledge from subject matter experts. Problems such as these not only occur in many different design and development settings, but also don't go away. Almost every project seems to be plagued by these constraints. Any experienced designer knows that he or she must accommodate time and cost restrictions and find a way to get usable knowledge from experts. Because such problems are commonly perceived as legitimate issues, it seems sensible to most practitioners to dedicate time to dealing with them in some way. Correspondingly, it is also sensible to researchers that these topics become part of the field's research agenda (Richey, 1997). If a predicament, even though critical to a given project, is not recurring, it is not likely to be perceived as an important research problem.

Some practitioner concerns, even though they be exasperating and confounding, are less easy to recognize as a potential research topic. For example, it is fairly typical for designers to be put in the position of having to regularly defend and promote the use of systematic procedures advocated by the field or to work to gain support for new innovations. Typically, these defenses are made to counter the resistance of managers with little design expertise. Is this dilemma a researchable problem, or is it instead simply a "hard fact of life" that everybody has to deal with (Cobb & Elder, 1983)? This problem could serve as a practitioner-generated incentive for design and development research. Whether such a topic would actually come to mind, however, is likely to depend upon whether the situation is defined in a way so that viable "solutions" are apparent (Elder & Cobb, 1984). This has occurred in our field when the emergence of widely available personal computers served as an impetus to the definition (or redefinition) of many problems, in areas such as project management, or learner control, or just-in-time learning. The problem was redefined because a possible solution was suddenly available.

Finally, what most people currently think is important influences the impact of practitioner-oriented research. Workplace problems that tend to command disciplinary attention are typically those that reflect the dominant thinking and ideas of the time. Even though such interest is highly variable and often specific to a given group of specialists, there are always topics that dominate the profession at any given time. Today, the "critical" problems related to evaluation of instructional programs and products are more likely to concern performance improvement and organizational impact rather than learning and individual impact. Three decades ago, formative evaluation problems that arose during the design and development process were the focus of many scholars in the field.

Clearly, one does not have to do everything in keeping with current trends. Innovation is difficult, or perhaps impossible, without independent thinking, and there are problems that are dormant and not generally recognized at a given time. However, the research that most successfully influences practice tends to conform to those broad areas of interest that are currently the focus of professional attention. In other words, the topics are timely and this interest is likely to be sustained. This ongoing timeliness is evidence of a particular topic being generally recognized as important to the discipline and often to society in general.

Representative workplace problems.   How has this problem-identification process actually worked with some completed projects that were rooted in workplace problems? Jones and Richey (2000), for example, conducted an in-depth examination of the use of rapid prototyping methods in natural work settings. The general problem was common to most design projects—that of being confronted with demands to generate high-quality products as well as to simultaneously reduce design and development time. Rapid prototyping methodologies have been suggested as one way of doing this, but most of the literature discusses these methods in abstract. This study sought to determine the nature of the *actual* use of rapid prototyping techniques by designers and customers and empirically describe the extent to which its use enhances traditional instructional design.

The problem of the Jones and Richey (2000) study was important because it:

- Addresses a common and recurring dilemma in many design and development projects.
- Tests the soundness and the practicality of one solution that is currently being suggested in the profession.

Another example of problems generated by the workplace involves the research of Sullivan, Ice, and Niedermeyer (2000). They were involved in the development and implementation of a comprehensive, K–12 energy-education curriculum over a 20-year period that was used by more than 12 million students in the United States. Here the "workplace" is K–12 educational settings across the country. Their research report describes the components of the program itself including instructional objectives, test items, and instructional materials, and provides guidelines for long-term instructional development projects.

The problems addressed by Sullivan, Ice, and Niedermeyer (2000) were important because:

- The curriculum in question is a new program used by many school districts.
- The scope of the program implementation is so large that the results become viable for many school districts.
- The long-term nature of the project provides an opportunity to examine retrospective data collected on many students from grades K–12.

Problems Related to Emerging Technology

Technology permeates our personal lives as well as that of the design and development profession. According to Milrad, Spector, and Davidsen (2000):

> Technology changes. Technology changes what we do and what we can do. People change on account of technology. Technology in support of learning and instruction is no different. Instructional technology changes what teachers and learners do and can do. (p. 13)

Today, many of the "cutting edge" research topics relate to the development and use of emerging technologies. Technology has always served as an impetus to design and development research with formal inquiry typically following the initial practical exploration and experimentation with new technologies.

But, fundamentally technology has captured the imagination of today's society. A recent review of the literature found that nearly half of the research studies on the development of products and tools dealt with computer-based or Web-based instruction (Richey, Klein, & Nelson, 2004). This is not surprising; Reiser (2002) asserts that in addition to the use of instructional design procedures the use of media and technology forms the core of our field.

Characteristics of technology problems.   What is the nature of research problems pertaining to technology-related design and development research? Typically the problems that are considered critical relate to:

- Emerging and innovative technology.
- The most effective techniques and tools for producing technology-based products.

In general, these issues center on how we can best take advantage of the potential of the new technologies.

While research focusing on technology does not have to deal only with innovative, emerging technologies, clearly these problems are typically the most interesting to practitioners and theorists alike. Of course, the notions of innovation vary. In the early years of our field, technology research was related to training films (Hoban, 1953; Lumsdaine, 1953), or motion pictures (Greenhill, 1955). Then television research (Kaner & Rosenstein, 1960) reflected the new technology. Newer applications of technology, such as language laboratories, continued to shape the field's technology research (Chomei & Houlihan, 1970). Today, the bulk of the technology-based research relates to advanced computer applications. The literature today includes many case studies that focus on the design and development of e-learning, Internet-based learning, and distance learning solutions. Some specific technologies are also being studied. For example, McLellan (2004) reviews a body of research literature devoted to virtual realities. In each of these situations, the topics of the research are advanced and forward-looking. Moreover, it is this very quality that facilitates perceptions of the relevance of the research, as well as contributes to the growing knowledge base of the field.

The questions that people have with respect to technology-based design and development are often simple: "How do you do it?" "What are the problems I can expect?" "How can I avoid them?" "What resources are needed?" Problems such as this tend to lend themselves to research on product development in which an actual project is documented and studied. Design and development research of this type does *not* typically stress learning issues, even though learning and performance are often evaluated. In other words, these problems are not of a media comparison nature (such as, Do learners achieve more using one type of teaching technology over another?) nor do they deal with characteristics of learners who are more successful using a particular technology (such as, the effects of attention span during instructional television). Instead, these are actual studies of how the product or program was designed, what conditions facilitate its development, or of what unique processes were used.

As computer technology has proliferated in society, it is not surprising that some attention is being directed toward the development of computer-based tools that are intended to streamline the design and development process. These tools can be used by both novice and expert designers. As a consequence, some technology-based design and development research focuses upon these tools. Efforts have been made to create design productivity tools, as well as tools that automate the entire design process. Some recent research has been conducted on the feasibility of creating and maintaining reusable, scaleable, and distributed content. Some of this research has been devoted to the definition and organization of "learning objects" or "knowledge objects" (Wiley, 2000; Zielinski, 2000).

The development of these tools and automated design processes can themselves be a focal point of research. These studies are similar in format to those studies that center upon the design and development of instructional materials. The problems again are "How are the tools or processes developed and used?" "What resources are needed?" "What problems may accompany their use?"

Other related studies can examine the use of the tools or processes in actual work settings. The critical problems here are, "Do the tools or procedures actually work?" "What designer skills are necessary?" "What work conditions facilitate their use?" "How can designers effectively and efficiently use them?"

Representative technology problems.　How has this problem identification process actually worked with some completed design and development research projects that were rooted in technology? What kinds of problems have been seen as critical? McKenney's (2002) dissertation, for example, examined the design of a computer program that supports the development of curriculum materials in secondary science and mathematics education in southern Africa. The research involved a careful and extensive documentation of the analysis, design, development, and evaluation of several prototypes of the computer program. This research problem was important because:

- It concerned the development of an innovative computerized design productivity tool.
- It has wide applicability.
- It has socially redeeming factors related to its use.

Another example relates to Web site development, a topic that is of much professional interest today. Corry, Frick, and Hansen (1997) conducted a study that involved the design and usability of a university Web site. The object was to identify ways of maximizing the usability of informational Web sites. They conducted a case study of the design processes and strategies implemented, which insured this usability. The topic of this study is important because:

- Web site design is a topic of great interest today and one in which many are involved.
- Its focus is upon usability rather than simple development.

Problems Related to Design and Development Theory

Many view instructional design as being "built upon the rock of instructional science" (Merrill, Drake, Lacy, Pratt, & the ID2 Research Group, 1996, p. 7). In keeping with this position, the evolution of design and development as a discipline requires that empirical evidence be collected to serve as the foundations of this science and of our theory.

Characteristics of theory-based problems. The design and development theory base is growing and becoming more diverse as the discipline expands. While the practice of instructional design itself rests upon many types of theory (principally systems theory, and theories of learning, instruction, and communication), instructional design theory tends to relate to ID models and processes, designer decision-making, and emerging areas in which ID principles and theories are being applied. These are the sources, in general, of theory-based design and development research problems. Within each of these theory clusters, more specific issues and problems emerge.

In 1981, Walter Dick wrote, "It may be argued that generic instructional design models represent the theory of instructional design. The theory includes a description of a series of steps which, when executed in sequence, result in predictable learning outcomes" (p. 29). This point-of-view is not inconsistent with that of Broderick (1963) who noted that then many used the term "model" as a synonym for "theory." While this view may not be accepted by everyone in the field today, ID models continue to serve as an important part of the theory base of the field, and as such provide direction for identifying design and development research problems. These problems tend to focus on

- A validation of ID models themselves.
- The study of particular elements and phases of the ID process.

Most ID models are procedural in nature. The majority of these procedural models pertain to comprehensive design projects, but some procedural models address more specific aspects of design and development processes. For example, there are models that speak to the selection and sequencing of specific learning activities, such as Gagné's Events of Instruction Model (Gagné, Wager, Golas, & Keller, 2005). There are motivation design models such as Keller's (1987) ARCS Model. There is van Merrienboer's model pertaining to designing instruction on complex cognitive skills (van Merrienboer & Dijkstra, 1997). These models serve as a stimulus to continuing research.

Problems surrounding the validation of these models are important targets of design and development research and are important to the substantiation of the design process. Without such research, ID processes are supported primarily by only user testimonials as evidence of their effectiveness. ID model validation can be viewed as either an internal validation of the components and process of the model, or as the external validation of the impact of the products of a model's use (Richey, 2005). Internal validation studies address problems such as:

- Are all steps included in the model necessary?
- Are the steps manageable in the prescribed sequence?
- To what extent does the model address all relevant environmental factors?
- To what extent is the model usable for a wide range of design projects and settings?
- Can the steps be completed efficiently under most working conditions?
- Is the use of this model cost effective?

External validation studies, on the other hand, address problems such as:

- To what extent does the resulting instruction meet learner needs, client needs, and client requirements?
- To what extent does the instruction result in efficient learning?
- To what extent do resulting behavior changes impact the organization's performance?

Other design and development studies concentrate on only one part of the design process—perhaps needs assessment or formative evaluation processes, for example. These investigations may also take the form of validations and address many of those concerns previously listed. However, they may be model explorations addressing problems such as:

- How is this ID phase implemented across settings and across projects? To what extent is it implemented?

- What resources are required?
- What is the impact of the products of this phase on the ID effort as a whole?

Another category of problems attuned to design and development research techniques concern the nature of designer thinking and decision making. Instructional design has been described as decision making, simulation, a creative activity, a scientific process, or "a very complicated act of faith" (Freeman, 1983, p. 3). In general, design and development is considered to be a form of problem solving, and research can address how designers approach the problem (e.g., the design task). Design and development studies of this nature deal with problems such as:

- How are design problems structured and solved? What decisions are made and when are they made?
- What are the differences in thinking and orientation among expert, experienced, and novice designers?
- What is the impact of other designer characteristics? For example, does gender impact designer decision-making?
- What is the impact of the design environment on the design task?

Representative theory problems.   How has this problem-identification process actually worked with some completed projects that were rooted in theory problems? Recently, there have been some model validation studies that follow the tenets of design and development research. Tracey (2002) constructed and validated an instructional systems design model that incorporated Gardner's notion of multiple intelligences. This study encompassed both an internal and external validation of the model. The external validation took place in a natural training setting. Tessmer, McCann, and Ludvigsen (1999) empirically tested the validity of a new model of needs assessment used to reassess existing training programs to determine if training excesses and deficiencies exist. This study included a partial internal validation and a formal external validation, again taking place in a "real" work environment. These two studies represent alternative approaches to model research. One addressed a model of the entire design and development process and the other examined one part of the process. They both addressed important research problems because the models in question were:

- New and untested.
- Based upon a firm theoretical foundation.
- Addressed a need in the field.

Perez and Emery's (1995) theory-based design and development research addresses issues of designer thinking. They sought to identify the differences in cognitive processing and problem-solving paths of expert and novice designers. The design task for each participant was controlled; each was presented with the same design task and was given a standard time limit. This study's problem was important because it attempted to:

- Determine actual design processes used.
- Understand the different thinking tactics used by persons of varying levels of design expertise.
- Relate the cognitive psychology research literature to the ID process.

USING THE LITERATURE TO IDENTIFY AND REFINE A RESEARCH PROBLEM

In the previous section, we suggested three sources of design and development research problems: (a) workplace settings and projects, (b) innovative technology, and (c) current and emerging theory in the field. In this section, we discuss how the literature can be used to identify and refine a research problem.

The Role of Literature in Problem Identification

The literature contains original ideas and concepts that form the collective body of prior work in a field (Tuckman, 1999). It provides a knowledge base for a researcher seeking important problems and questions. For example, an article published in a journal aimed at practitioners may stimulate an idea related to the use of design and development in the workplace, or a paper presented at a conference may suggest possible questions about the design of technology-based instruction. The discussion section of research reports is a good source for potential problems and questions as they often give "directions for future research."

The literature also offers information to help a researcher refine his or her problem statement and questions. According to Gall, Gall, and Borg (2003) you should conduct a thorough study of the literature after identifying a potential research problem to answer the following questions:

- Has research on this problem been previously conducted?
- If so, what has been learned?

- What can this study contribute to what is already known?
- Is the research problem significant or are there more important problems that should be addressed?

Furthermore, the literature can suggest ideas for research procedures, data sources, and instruments. For example, a well-written research article on the validity of an ID model might recommend the range of participants or data collection tools to include in another validation study.

Sources for a Literature Review in Design and Development

Researchers should consult a variety of sources for literature in their field of study. Patten (2002) suggests several general sources to identify broad problem areas including textbooks, review and reference publications, "signature" publications of major professional associations, and journals that specialize in research reviews. These are always good places to find ideas for research. However, what sources are available to someone who is interested in conducting design and development research?

Traditional sources of literature. Journals that publish articles on research, theory, development, and utilization of instructional design and technology (IDT) provide a primary source of literature. They contain original ideas and material that can be used in a literature review. According to Klein and Rushby (2007) journals in our field focus on a wide variety of topics, including distance education, instructional development, multimedia, and performance improvement. These authors describe 75 journals in IDT and related fields. Table 2–1 contains a list of some journals that may be of interest to those conducting design and development research.

Other traditional sources of literature are books and journals that publish review and synthesis articles. For example, the various editions of the *Handbook of Research on Educational Communications and Technology* (edited by Jonassen, 1996, 2004) is an excellent resource to find information on topics of interest to a design and development researcher; the *Handbook of Human Performance Technology* (edited by Stolovitch & Keeps, 1999) provides information on the processes, tools, and interventions of performance improvement. Furthermore, *Review of Research in Education* contains articles that interpret and synthesize educational research from a wide range of disciplines.

Finally, textbooks are a traditional source that should not be overlooked when you are conducting a review of the literature. For example, textbooks such as *Instructional Design Theories and Models* (edited by Reigeluth, 1999)

TABLE 2–1.
Journals Relating to Design & Development Research

American Journal of Distance Education
Australian Journal of Educational Technology
British Journal of Educational Technology
Canadian Journal of Learning and Technology
Educational Technology Magazine
Educational Technology Research and Development
Instructional Science
International Journal of Educational Technology
International Journal of Training and Development
International Journal of Training Research
Journal of Distance Education
Journal of Educational Computing Research
Journal of Educational Technology Systems
Journal of Instruction Delivery Systems
Journal of Interactive Instruction Development
Journal of Interactive Learning Research
Journal of the Learning Sciences
Journal of Research on Technology in Education
Journal of Technology, Learning, and Assessment
Learning and Instruction
Performance Improvement Journal
Performance Improvement Quarterly
Quarterly Review of Distance Education
Tech Trends Magazine
Training Magazine

and *Trends and Issues in Instructional Design and Technology* (edited by Reiser & Dempsey, 2007) examine current and emerging ideas in the field.

Dissertations. While journals and books provide the foundation for a literature review, some of them may not have the most current or "cutting edge" information. It is not unusual for an author to submit a manuscript for publication, only to see it take two or more years before it's reviewed, revised, and finally published. This process of "refereed publication" helps to ensure the quality of scholarship in a field. It also increases the length of time it takes before a new, emerging process or technology is exposed to a field.

Recently completed dissertations provide a good source of up-to-date information on workplace issues, emerging technologies, innovative tools, and promising ID models. A well-written dissertation also provides a comprehensive review of literature on a topic (but we caution you not to rely on secondary sources alone). Furthermore, a well-constructed dissertation may include complete data sets that often must be left out of subsequent publications since journals do not provide enough space for detailed documentation of design and development research data (Richey & Klein, 2005).

An excellent resource for locating dissertations is *Dissertation Abstracts International*, which offers an online database you can use to search over 2 million entries (http://www.umi.com/umi/dissertations/). Studies in education are categorized into 35 topic areas including technology (as of this writing, 12,205 titles related to this topic were included). A good source for finding dissertations that have employed a design and development research approach is the online database, *Doctoral Research in Educational Technology: A Directory of Dissertations*, a compilation of completed doctoral dissertation studies in the IDT field (http://www.cortland.edu/education/dissdir/).

Conference papers. Papers presented at conferences of professional associations also offer information on new ideas and trends in a field. However, many conference papers are not subjected to a rigorous peer-review process. Klein and Rushby (2007) point out, "as an educated consumer of information, you should critically analyze the content of what you read regardless of where it has been published" (p. 262).

In many cases, full-text conference papers are not distributed at the presentation itself, and often those papers that are distributed do not include empirical data. One way to obtain a complete paper is to send a message to the author requesting a copy of the paper and any others the author has written on the topic. We also suggest that you examine the contents of a convention program for topics and papers of interest, even if you didn't attend the conference. Many learned societies now post searchable conference programs on their Web sites.

Some professional associations publish collections of selected conference papers, known as *proceedings*. For example, the Association for Educational Communications and Technology (http://www.aect.org) publishes the *Annual Proceedings of Selected Research and Development Papers*. The Association for the Advancement of Computing in Education (http://www.aace.org) has a digital library that includes conference proceedings related to educational technology and e-learning. These resources are useful to researchers focused on a design and development topic.

Documents from work settings. We previously identified the workplace as a primary source of design and development research problems. Correspondingly, documents from work settings can contribute to the knowledge base of the researcher who is constructing design and development research questions. They can also be used as data sources to answer these research questions. For example, needs assessment reports, detailed design documents, memoranda that summarize meetings with clients, and evaluation reports can be reviewed to search for important issues and problems. While the proprietary nature of such documents and artifacts can pose a special challenge for researchers, many researchers have secured similar documents with pledges to maintain anonymity and confidentiality.

FOCUSING THE DESIGN AND DEVELOPMENT RESEARCH PROBLEM

Once an important problem has been identified, the next task is to focus the problem in such a way that the research effort can lead to specific new knowledge for the field. This focusing process gives the study a "design and development twist," and narrows it so that new findings can be attributed to particular aspect of the complex design and development process.

Transforming Research Problems into Research Questions

While there are some unique focusing strategies used in design and development research, as with all research, the focusing process ultimately results in a set of research questions that reflect the critical components of the problem selected for study. This involves a process of transforming a general topic into specific questions[1] that frame the study. In this process, the research topic is narrowed. Figure 2–1 summarizes this narrowing process.

Once an area of interest and the problem have been identified using the techniques discussed earlier in this chapter, the narrowing task has just begun. This process involves determining the various components of the problem. If you are going to study the use of automated design tools, for instance, what are the critical parts of the problem? Should you concentrate on the type of content typically addressed using these tools? What is the expertise of the designer using the tool? What are the attitudes of the designer toward automation? What are the available resources? The knowledge needed to identify the important parts of the problem situation comes primarily from your command of the literature, your familiarity with the problem, and your familiarity with the research context.

---

[1]While some design and development research studies are built around formal hypotheses, the more common approach is to form research questions since there is seldom a research base in the literature that is sufficiently substantial to justify hypothesis formulation. In addition, design and development research often utilizes qualitative designs that are typically based upon research questions instead of hypotheses.

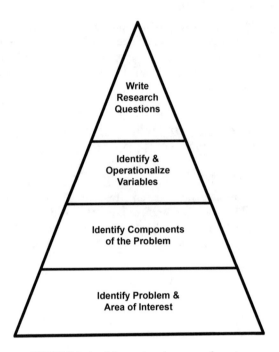

FIGURE 2–1.   Narrowing the research topic.

Next, these components need to be identified as specific variables such as designer expertise or attitude toward the tool. Variables are those things that are "thought to influence (or to be influenced by) a particular state of being in something else" (Hoover & Donovan, 1995, p. 21). Variables have mutually exclusive categories; participants in a research study vary in terms of the categories to which they belong (Patten, 2004). They form the crux of your study and will become the heart of your research questions.

In the above example, you might eventually use your variables to form a research question such as, "What is the relationship between designer expertise and perceptions of the XYZ automated design system's ease of use?" Or you might have a question which, while still narrow, is much more open such as, "What conditions facilitate the effective use of the XYZ automated design system?" The construction of a good question is a critical component of planning a research study. However, research questions are not complete until all the variables included have been clearly defined. This is done by constructing operational definitions of terms.

According to Wallen and Fraenkel (2001), "operational definitions require that a researcher specify the actions or operations required to measure or identify the term" (p. 16). Consider this research question again: "What is the relationship between designer expertise and perceptions of the XYZ automated design system's ease of use?" How should you operationally define the variable "designer expertise?" Is an expert designer someone with formal education in ID or someone with 10 or more years of professional experience (or both)? Alternatively, does designer expertise relate to the quality of products developed or the impact those products have on learners? Furthermore, how will you define the variable "ease of use"? Is the automated system easier to use if designers spend less time or mental effort when using it?

Identifying a research problem and its components, identifying and operationalizing variables, and writing research questions are critical components of planning empirical research. The task of planning also requires thoughtful consideration of the parameters of your design and development study.

Determining the Parameters of the Study

The problem definition stage also includes establishing the parameters of the particular research project. Establishing these parameters is a part of focusing the study.

General parameter decisions.   One must make some standard decisions when determining the parameters of any design and development study. These include:

- Will all phases of the design and development cycle be addressed, or will the research concentrate on just one particular aspect of the process?
- Will the research be conducted while design and development activities are *occurring* or will retrospective data be collected on an instructional program or performance intervention that was *previously* designed and developed? Or will one consider both options?

Other parameter decisions, however, vary depending upon whether one is conducting research on a product, tool, or model.

Parameters of research on product and tool design and development.   Much design and development research is conducted during the design of a product or tool. When establishing the parameters of this type of study, the following considerations should be addressed:

- What will be the scope of the study? Will it address the analysis of learning needs and goals? Will it address the planning and production of interventions, materials, and activities? Will it address the tryout and revision of these materials and activities?

- Will evaluation data be collected and reported? Will formative, summative, and/or confirmative evaluation be conducted?
- Will enroute and outcome measures be used? Will student-student, student-teacher, or student-technology interactions be investigated? Will reaction, learning, performance, or return on investment be measured?

The parameters of research on design and development models.   Research may involve constructing and validating unique design models and processes, as well identifying those conditions that facilitate their successful use. When one is establishing the parameters of this type of design and development study, the following decisions must be made:

- Will the study address model development, model implementation or model validation, or a combination of these phases?
- Will the study encompass data from one design and development project or many?
- Will the design and development tasks being studied be situation specific or will the tasks encompass a variety of design settings?

LOOKING AHEAD

This chapter has focused on how to start planning your design and development research project by identifying appropriate topics and questions. We provided some guidelines for selecting a research problem and suggested several sources for design and development research questions. We also discussed how to refine and focus a research problem and gave several sources for finding literature related to design and development. On the next page, we have provided a checklist to help identify and focus your design and development research problem.

Once a researchable problem is identified and refined, the next step is to design your research study. This requires the delineation of concrete research procedures. What methods of inquiry are used in design and development research? What research designs are appropriate for the various types of design and development studies? What research design problems are common in design and development studies? These issues will be addressed in the next chapter.

A CHECKLIST FOR IDENTIFYING AND FOCUSING THE PROBLEM IN A DESIGN AND DEVELOPMENT STUDY

1. Identify a topic of interest and a research problem from one or more of the following areas—the workplace, emerging technology, or design and development theory.
2. Evaluate the research problem by answering the following questions:
   - Is the problem in the mainstream of the field?
   - Is it important and timely?
   - Is there a substantial body of literature in the area?
   - Do you have the knowledge, skill, expertise, interest and resources necessary to study it?
3. Conduct a thorough review of the literature related to the research problem using a variety of sources.
4. Narrow the focus of the research problem by answering the following questions:
   - Will the study focus on a product, tool, or model?
   - Which components of the problem will be studied?
   - What variables will be studied?
   - What are the operational definitions of these variables?
5. Write specific research questions.
6. Establish the parameters and scope of the study by answering the following questions:
   - Which design and development phases and activities will be addressed?
   - What types of data will be collected?
   - Will the study be situation-specific or will it encompass a variety of settings?

3

Design and Development Research Methodology

A standard question of novice researchers is "What's the hardest part of doing research?" One realistic reply is "Whatever you're working on at the time." Problem definition is a complex task, but that should be accomplished by now. The next major quandary is determining what methods and strategies you will use to produce meaningful data and insightful conclusions—in other words, constructing the research design. In design and development research, as with other types of research, this, too, can be a difficult undertaking.

A good research design makes it possible for you to answer the questions posed by the research problem or test the hypothesized solutions to the problem. A good design makes it possible to determine how the findings can be applied in other situations. A faulty research design, on the other hand, produces data that is suspect, which ultimately leads to unsubstantiated conclusions that have little likelihood of being used in practice situations. Poor research designs make the research process a waste of time. In this chapter we will:

- Explore the nature of research design.
- Describe the characteristics of design and development research methodology.
- Provide a strategy for matching research questions and methodology.

We will examine specific design and development research methods and strategies in the following two chapters.

THE NATURE OF RESEARCH DESIGN

Similar to designing instruction and other types of interventions, designing research is a planning process. Research designs have been called the blueprints that guide researchers throughout their projects (Frankfort-Nachmias & Nachmias, 2000). A research design establishes the general framework of a study, addressing each phase of the investigative process. However, research designs are not rigid prescriptions for completing a study. Expert researchers design their studies and then implement these designs with flexibility as they respond to situations that arise as their projects progress.

Research designs vary depending to a great extent upon whether the study has a quantitative or qualitative orientation. Nonetheless, there are some general concerns that should be considered when designing any research project. These include:

- Establishing the validity of the final conclusions.
- Establishing conditions that make causal inferences and assertions plausible.
- Facilitating generalization and interpretation.
- Anticipating problems that may arise in the course of conducting the research.

Establishing Validity

The key undertaking in research design is to establish conditions that will enable one to make valid conclusions as a result of the research process. With respect to quantitative research, this is fundamentally a matter of establishing both internal and external validity of the study's resulting data. Campbell and Stanley's (1963) landmark chapter "Experimental and Quasi-Experimental Designs for Research" delineates the various threats to such validity and describes ways to manage these flaws.[1] Internal validity can be put at risk by history or maturational effects, or statistical regression, for example. One instance of the effects of history that occurred in our field was determining how to

---

[1] Readers who are unfamiliar with threats to validity are encouraged to read the 1963 Campbell and Stanley chapter that has been reprinted by Houghton Mifflin Company and is currently available.

account for the implications of layoff notices that were issued during the study of a training program. External validity can also be compromised by a variety of factors, such as the interactive effects of pretests or multiple treatments.

Establishing validity for qualitative research is also critical but relies upon different approaches. Here validity may be insured by procedures such as eliminating selection bias, correcting biased inferences, or increasing the number of observations, (King, Keohane, & Verba, 1994). For example, how can you contain the risks of interviewing employees who have been recommended to participate in the research by their supervisors?

Establishing validity depends upon one's command of a variety of research methods. You need to have skills in areas such as constructing a sound experiment, or planning and conducting interviews. These are the general skills of a researcher, the skills that we assume you have already acquired prior to taking on a design and development research project.

Facilitating Notions of Causality

Research designs (especially quantitative designs) are concerned with three key issues that make it possible to conclude that independent and dependent variables are causally related: comparison, manipulation, and control (Frankfort-Nachmias & Nachmias, 2000). Many methodologies are attuned to the desire to determine whether the relationship between two variables is causal or not. What media or teaching techniques promote learning? What is the impact of a particular performance intervention on organizational improvement? Designs are constructed to find the answers to these questions.

Manipulation in the classic experimental design involves establishing controlled treatment and non-treatment situations to determine causality. The researcher controls the situation by determining what the treatment is, who gets it, and insuring that the changes occur only after the activation of the treatment. Other extraneous factors in the setting also must be controlled to isolate the treatment effects.

The effort to determine causality is not entirely the domain of quantitative research. Qualitative forms of inquiry are also concerned with causality, but in a somewhat different manner. Qualitative researchers typically expand their explanations of causality to include notions of *multiple* causality and expand their methods to encompass ways of making causal *inferences* rather than assertions (King et al., 1994). While there is typically no manipulation in a qualitative design, qualitative researchers are also concerned with control. They, too, must insure that their observations are made without error and that they have not omitted any data related to a variable that might provide either descriptive or explanatory information that is critical to the question at hand (King et al., 1994). This involves establishing procedures that control the research process and to interjecting biases into the observations. In qualitative research, however, the research settings typically are not under the control of the researcher, and the events and activities are naturally occurring.

Facilitating Generalization and Interpretation

Quantitative research designs seek to establish external validity so that the findings of a particular study can be generalized to a larger population. The value of the research often lies in the extent to which this occurs. Will the rules for visual message design apply to all instructional situations, for example, or only to those dealing with children of certain backgrounds? The population to which the results should be generalized is identified early in the process and then random sampling strategies are employed to insure a representative group of participants. Researchers also take steps to insure that their research settings closely reflect the settings to which they want to generalize.

Qualitative researchers, on the other hand, often question the value of generalization because they feel that in doing so the findings must by necessity be stripped of their contextual richness (Patton, 1987). In addition, there are also issues with the extent to which small sample research findings can be generalized. For example, do the findings of a study on how designers in a health care organization conduct needs assessment apply to other settings or can the results only be understood in light of the resources, constraints, and climate of the particular organization? Qualitative researchers typically employ purposeful sampling techniques to insure information-rich data. It is felt that these techniques, combined with careful non-biased observations, can lead to sound interpretation and inference even from small samples. Such conclusions are often the primary goal of qualitative researchers, rather than aiming to generalize their conclusions to a broad population.

Anticipating and Avoiding Problems

Research design is a process of anticipating everything that will happen during a study. This is a large task that involves more than simply applying the various methodological techniques. It also means engaging in a process of anticipating the problems that you will encounter, of determining how to get around these obstacles, and in general, figuring out how to minimize error in your study. These activities rely on more than your capacity to make reasoned and informed judgments based upon technical and subject-matter knowledge. They depend upon knowing enough about the research setting to enable you to make design decisions based upon your imagination, intuition, and knowledge of the customs of the community (Hoover & Donovan, 1995).

Specific procedures must be devised to compensate for these anticipated problems. For example, one study focused upon using special strategies to engage at-risk male high-school students. The treatment took a total of 10 days to administer. One might logically select a two-week period during the school year for the data collection. However, someone who knows the setting well would realize that absenteeism is high on Fridays and Mondays. Therefore, the study was not conducted on these days. Most research that takes place in natural settings is filled with potential pitfalls such as these. It is the researcher's job to prepare for them.

Components of a Research Design

Researchers struggle with a myriad of problems when constructing their research designs. Their solutions to these problems depend upon both technical and intuitive analyses. Typically, a comprehensive research design describes the decisions that have been made with respect to:

- The types of observations that will be required to answer the research questions or test the hypotheses, that is the data collection that will be necessary.
- The strategies that will be used to make these observations, that is the research methods that will be employed.
- Variables that are central to the study and variables that should be controlled.
- The participants in the research project.
- Instrumentation and measurement of variables.
- Data analysis.

The remainder of this chapter will focus on the general methods typically employed in design and development research. The specific strategies used in product and tool research and model research will be discussed in the following chapters, as will issues surrounding the selection of participants, instrumentation and data collection, and, lastly, interpreting and reporting the data.

THE CHARACTERISTICS OF DESIGN AND DEVELOPMENT RESEARCH METHODOLOGY

Design and development research is an umbrella term for the study of design and development using a broad collection of traditional methods and strategies, both quantitative and qualitative. Which methods you select and how these methods are employed are dependent not only upon the nature of the research problem and questions, but also upon whether you are doing product and tool research or model research.

Commonly Used Design and Development Methods and Strategies

Design and development research uses a wide variety of methodologies. Much design and development research—both product and tool research and model research—relies upon a variety of qualitative techniques, including case studies, interviews, document reviews, and observations. Evaluation research techniques (both qualitative and quantitative) are also included in many studies that focus on product and tool development. Model development and use studies often employ survey research techniques, while model validation studies frequently use traditional experimental designs. Some of the most commonly used design and development research methods are shown in Table 3–1.

The list in Table 3–1 is certainly not exhaustive, but it does represent the methods most commonly used in design and development research. There

TABLE 3–1.
Common Methods Employed in Design and Development Research

Type of Research	Project Emphasis	Research Methods Employed
Product & Tool Research	Comprehensive Design & Development Projects	Case Study, Content Analysis, Evaluation, Field Observation, In-Depth Interview
Product & Tool Research	Phases of Design & Development	Case Study, Content Analysis, Expert Review, Field Observation, In-Depth Interview, Survey
Product & Tool Research	Tool Development & Use	Evaluation, Expert Review, In-Depth Interview, Survey
Model Research	Model Development	Case Study, Delphi, In-Depth Interview, Literature Review, Survey, Think-Aloud Methods
Model Research	Model Validation	Experimental, Expert Review, In-Depth Interview
Model Research	Model Use	Case Study, Content Analysis, Field Observation, In-Depth Interview, Survey, Think-Aloud Methods

are even examples of historical research (e.g., Gay & Mazur, 1993) and philo-sophical inquiry (e.g., Luiz, 1983) that have been employed in design and development studies. However, these methodologies are not common.

If you look at the larger body of design and development research litera-ture, there are some key conclusions that can be drawn with respect to their research designs. First, these studies tend to rely more on qualitative techniques than on quantitative techniques. Perhaps this is because design and develop-ment projects and processes resist the control imposed by many quantitative research orientations. Perhaps it is because the wide range of projects demands exploratory techniques. The use of qualitative methods is not required in design and development research, but it does tend to be widespread.

Next, if you look at the design and development research literature, you will find that the studies tend to deal more with real-life projects, rather than with simulated or contrived projects. This certainly distinguishes design and devel-opment research from other types of research in the field. Sometimes the pro-jects are currently underway during the research; at other times they are sim-ply being recalled and reported on. Design and development research is always applied research and related to the practice of ID, rather than the examination of isolated variables. We know of no design and development research that could be classified as basic research.

Lastly, if you look at the design and development research literature, you'll find that most studies used many research methods. For example, Visser, Plomp, Amirault, and Kuiper (2002) describe a product-development study that used both qualitative and quantitative strategies including interviews, content analysis, surveys, and experiments. Not only are many types of research meth-ods used across design and development studies, but it is also common for researchers to employ multiple methods in the same study, capitalizing on the best features of each. Rarely do you find a simple experiment being conducted or only one survey being administered, for example. You can find such studies in the literature, but it is not the norm.

Mixed and Multiple Methods Research

Because so many methods are typically used, design and development research tends to be complex. Often the methods used span both qualitative and quan-titative strategies. A design and development study may depend upon both field observations of designers as they follow a given model, for example, and then a survey of many developers to determine the extent to which others followed the procedures of the original targeted group.

The term "mixed methods research" has been used to describe those studies that combine qualitative and quantitative methods. This is a way of using mul-tiple approaches to answer given research questions. Ross and Morrison (2004) support this trend when they take the position that "quantitative and qualitative approaches are more useful when used together than when either is used alone . . . [and] when combined, are likely to yield a richer and more valid understanding" (p. 1039).

An example of a mixed method approach is a study by Plummer, Gillis, Legree, and Sanders (1992) who used two research methodologies—case study and experimental—in conjunction with an ID task. This project involved a study of the development of a job aid used by the military when operating a complicated piece of communications equipment. The experimental phase was an evaluation of the job aid in the effectiveness of the job aid was studied. Three instructional situations were compared: (a) using the job aid alone, (b) using it in combination with a demonstration, and (c) using the technical manual in combination with a demonstration. Consequently, not only was impact information secured, but information relating to the superior conditions for using the newly developed product was also obtained.

The quantitative and qualitative methodological perspectives are not at odds theoretically or philosophically. Johnson and Onwuegbuzie (2004) describe the areas of current agreement between advocates of both positions:

- While individual perceptions are affected by one's background experience, these are not different realities, but simply varying perceptions.
- It is possible for one data set to be compatible with different theories, i.e., there are alternative explanations of phenomena.
- There is not always final proof in empirical research.
- Researchers are bound by their values, attitudes, and beliefs.

These fundamental agreements make mixed method research not only practical in many situations, but also logically sound.

However, many design and development studies that employ multiple research methods are not mixing the quantitative and qualitative orientations. They are simply making use of a variety of similar strategies. They may be studying product development by conducting in-depth interviews, as well as conducting field observations as did Corry, Frick, and Hansen (1997). Or they may be validating a model by using a Delphi study and then following up with an experiment that tests one model with another as did Tracey (2002).

MATCHING RESEARCH METHODS
AND QUESTIONS

The question then is, "What are the best research methods to employ in a given design and development study?" Fundamentally, this decision should be driven by the study's research questions rather than one's own biases or philosophical orientations. There are various approaches to deciding on a methodology. The following is one approach.

Classifying Design and Development Research Goals

First, cluster your research questions or hypotheses in terms of their general purpose. All research can be viewed as being exploratory, descriptive, or explanatory. Singleton and Straits (2005) describe these distinctions. Exploratory research relates to topics about which very little is known. Because of this, there are few guidelines to follow and the research designs are less structured than in descriptive research. These studies tend to be qualitative research. Descriptive research is more of a "fact-finding enterprise, focusing on relatively few dimensions of a well-defined entity" (p. 68). It can be either quantitative or qualitative in nature. Lastly, explanatory studies are initiated not only to describe phenomena, but also to test relationships between elements of the problem. They are typically designed to "seek the answers to problems and hypotheses" (p. 69). These studies usually employ quantitative methods.

There are many examples of exploratory, descriptive, and explanatory design and development research. Much of the product and tool research building upon advanced technological delivery systems is exploratory since it is relatively uncharted territory. For example, McKenney and van den Akker's (2005) research highlights the processes and principles used in constructing a computer-based tool for curriculum development. There is also a body of descriptive research that systematically records the way specific design phases are implemented. Twitchell, Holton, and Trott's (2000) survey research focusing on evaluation is one example, and Cowell's (2001) needs assessment research using in-depth interview techniques is another. Richey's (1992) studies, on the other hand, would be considered explanatory research. Here, large-scale survey data were used to identify those factors that were predictive of changes in knowledge, attitudes, and performance following corporate safety training experiences.

Many studies, however, have multiple purposes. Consequently, there are research questions or hypotheses that are classified in different categories. These studies are likely to employ mixed or multiple research methods.

Matching Research Purposes and Methods

After classifying your research questions, you can then (a) relate them to the general focus of your research, such as comprehensive product development studies, tool use studies, or model validation studies, and (b) select an appropriate research methodology. Table 3–2 shows typical research methods that

TABLE 3–2.
Representative Matches between Purposes, Methods and Types of Design and Development Research

Purpose of Research	Common Research Methods	Type of Research
Exploratory	Case Study Content Analysis Field Observation In-Depth Interview Mixed Methods Multiple Methods	• Product Development • ID Phases • Tool Development & Use • Model Development • Model Use
	Literature Review & Analysis	• Model Development • Tool Development & Use
	Think-Aloud Methods	• Product Development • Model Development • Model Use
Descriptive	Content Analysis In-Depth Interview Survey Mixed Methods Multiple Methods	• Product Development • ID Phases • Tool Development & Use • Model Development • Model Validation • Model Use
	Case Study Evaluation	• Product Development • Program Development • ID Phases • Tool Development & Use
	Expert Review	• Product Development • ID Phases • Tool Development & Use • Model Development • Model Validation (Internal)
	Delphi	• Model Development • Model Validation (Internal)
Explanatory	Experimental	• Product Development • Tool Development & Use • Model Validation (External)
	Evaluation	• Product Development • Program Development • Tool Development & Use • Model Validation (External)
	Survey	• Tool Development & Use • Model Validation (Internal)

are employed in design and development projects falling into the exploratory, descriptive, and explanatory research groupings.

Explanatory design and development research tends to employ experimental designs, or evaluation techniques, or use surveys. This is fairly clear cut. Descriptive and exploratory studies often use the same methodologies, but their use varies in terms of the type of design and development research being conducted. Almost any type of design and development study can use interviews, for example. Sometimes the interview methodology is used for exploratory purposes and others for descriptive purposes. Delphi techniques, on the other hand, tend to be confined to descriptive model development or validation studies. Literature reviews are used as research techniques typically for model development and tool-development studies that are exploratory in nature, and "think aloud" methods are always used in exploratory studies.

As you think of your own future research, keep in mind that Table 3–2 should be merely a guide to your thinking. Each study is unique. Methods may be legitimately used for other purposes than those shown in this table. Research design is a large scale problem-solving activity that demands analytical thinking skills, technical knowledge, creativity, and ingenuity. The next two chapters describe typical methods and strategies that have been used in actual design and development studies. These examples may also help you select your own methods and strategies.

LOOKING AHEAD

You should now have some idea about what research design is all about and what kinds of methods are used in design and development research. In this chapter, we explored the nature of research design and discussed some general concerns that should be addressed when designing any research project. We have also provided some strategies for matching research questions to methods. We offer a checklist on the next page to help you identify and select an appropriate methodology to address your design and development research questions.

However, there is more to learn about these topics. In the next two chapters we will look specifically at the kind of research methods and strategies used in product and tool research and model research. First, we will examine product and tool studies to see how they have been designed. What techniques do researchers use to design sound studies that can lead to valid conclusions that are useful to both scholars and practitioners?

A CHECKLIST FOR MATCHING DESIGN AND DEVELOPMENT RESEARCH QUESTIONS AND METHODS

1. Identify the general purpose of your design and development study by classifying the research questions as exploratory, descriptive or explanatory.
2. Identify those research methodologies commonly used in design and development studies with a similar purpose.
3. Select one or more methodologies appropriate to your study's purpose and research questions.

4

Product and Tool Research: Methods and Strategies

Many design and development studies focus on a specific product or program. Frequently, this type of research examines the entire design and development process from analyses to evaluation. However, some of this research concentrates only on one or two phases of design and development. Furthermore, researchers have recently examined the development and use of tools that can be used to assist designers and developers or support the teaching/learning process. In studies of products, programs, and tools, there is a tendency to combine the tasks of doing design and development and studying it.

In this chapter, we will examine the research methods and strategies used in representative product, program, and tool studies, research related to:

- Product and program development.
- The various phases of design and development.
- The development and use of tools.

STRATEGIES OF PRODUCT
DEVELOPMENT RESEARCH

The classic product development study is descriptive research using case study methods. Many of these studies describe the entire lifespan of the product development process in detail (see Russell, 1990 or Shellnut, Knowlton, & Savage, 1999). These projects provide an extensive description of design and development, as well as pertinent technological details. If you were planning a product development study, it would be useful to examine reports of similar efforts found in both dissertations (such as the Russell study) and journal articles (such as the Shellnut et al. study).

The design and development literature contains many descriptions of new products, but there is a scarcity of articles that report on the systematic collection of data on design and development processes in such a way that would allow others to replicate them. The two studies that we will examine here serve as both examples and models of product development research. Visser, Plomp, Amirault, and Kuiper (2002) is a design and development product study, describing the project from its initial pilot study through a yearlong tryout and evaluation of the product. The Corry, Frick, and Hansen (1997) study is more limited in scope. This research concerns the development of a Web site, especially emphasizing techniques for formative evaluation and usability testing.

A Representative Mixed Methods
Case Study

Visser et al.'s (2002) research culminated in an instructional product that was designed to be used in conjunction with other distance education materials. Specifically, they designed, developed, and tested a technique for creating motivational messages. This approach has been called the Motivational Messages Support System (Visser, 1998).[1] The product attends to learners' motivational requirements and, in turn, is intended to reduce the dropout and noncompletion rates of distance education programs.

The research design of Visser et al. provides for a systematic process of data collection that results first in a prototype of the final product. Then, throughout the study, the design allows for continued "development and the improvement of the product (the motivational message), focused on the process and assessed the validity, the practicality and the effectiveness of the product"

---

[1]It is not unusual for design and development research to originate as a dissertation study. This is one example. For a more complete description of the study, readers are directed to Visser (1998), the dissertation report that describes the project from inception and piloting through design, development, tryout, and cost-effectiveness evaluation. Information from both the dissertation and the journal article are used as a basis of this research-design description.

(Visser, 1998, p. 17). The entire product development effort was an empirical process.

The main study was preceded by a pilot study designed to identify the characteristics of effective motivational messages and to develop a prototype of such a message. The pilot study included 17 international student participants in one distance education course. Data were collected from student records, interviews with program staff, and end-of-course questionnaires. Analyses of these data led to (a) a student motivational profile, (b) a series of eight motivational messages delivered via the mail, (c) evidence of message effectiveness, and (d) an increase in course completion rate. Thus, the pilot study provided evidence of the soundness of the basic approach. The researcher served as the course instructor in the pilot study.

The main study was extended to 81 students enrolled in five distance education courses, two using personalized motivational messages, two using collective motivational messages, and one using no motivational messages. Each course was considered as a separate one-year case study. Here, the researcher was the instructor of only one course; consequently, she assumed the more traditional role of observer, but still had multiple roles in the research. She was the product developer, the researcher, and the instructor.

The researcher trained participating instructors in the use of motivational messages and gave them a structured implementation plan (either for personalized or collective messages) to follow during the course of the year of study. The instructors selected for the study had no preferences or biases in terms of project outcomes. The instructors developed the motivational messages for their own courses according to the structured plan. A variety of data-collection instruments were used in addition to those used in the pilot study. Student-related data were collected with pre- and post-course questionnaires, and telephone interviews. Instructors provided existing course-completion records, questionnaires, course logbooks, and time-monitoring sheets, and then had in-depth interviews with the researcher.

These data enabled the researchers to determine if motivational messages were effective and efficient, and which types of messages were superior. The entire study combined elements of exploratory, descriptive, and explanatory research. While the study would be generally classified as a case study (one supported by a pilot study), it is a good example of a mixed methods approach. It includes both qualitative strategies (case study, interview, content analysis) and quantitative strategies (survey, experiment).

A Representative Multiple Qualitative Methods Study

Corry, Frick, and Hansen's (1997) study pertains to the design of a new university Web site, with a special focus on the Web site's usability as a student-recruiting mechanism. The project began with an extensive needs assessment based upon in-depth interviews of persons from 35 campus offices to determine the university's most frequently asked questions. Over 300 questions were identified, and were subsequently clustered into 30 question categories which were then reduced to six categories that served as the basis for the prototype Web design. Questions and categories were worded in keeping with interviewee's language rather than official university nomenclature. Paper designs of the first prototype Web site included a homepage, six second-level satellite pages, and one section of third-level satellite pages.

This type of project-specific procedural detail is typical of product development studies. The research design here is a blend of data-collection techniques and the design and development procedures themselves. Often studies will also provide details of exactly how the product is developed, although it was not done in this particular research report. In this case, the report would have described how the Web site was designed and developed.

The usability testing involved paper copies of both the university's existing Web site and the prototype of the proposed Web site. Hypertext links were underlined. Twenty-one persons were involved in determining how quickly and efficiently answers could be found to the common questions identified in the needs assessment. Participants included current and potential students and their parents, as well as university faculty, staff, and alumni.

The participants were asked to answer given questions using only one page of the sample Web sites at a time. They could use the underlined words to help them move from page to page. Participants were asked to "think aloud" while they were finding the answers; they were to describe what they were thinking as they solved the problem. A practice item was worked through prior to the actual task. Participants answered 15–20 questions using the existing Web site, and another 15–20 questions using the revised Web site. The Web site order was reversed for half of the participants. While the participants were working, researchers collected the following data: (a) problem areas, (b) time devoted to each task, and (c) any Web site paths followed.

The new Web site proved to be more effective and efficient than the original one. However, revisions were made to this new Web site as a result of the initial usability testing. The revised Web site was then tested with 16 persons following the same procedures previously used. The data gathered from this test resulted in further revisions. Finally the production version underwent additional user testing and there were even more refinements made to the Web site.

Corry, Frick, and Hansen (1997) is an example of a product development study that is primarily exploratory in nature, and it demonstrates how design and development can be empirically based. This study employed multiple qualitative research methods: field observation, think-aloud methods, and in-depth interviews.

STRATEGIES OF PROGRAM
DEVELOPMENT RESEARCH

While much product development research focuses on specific instructional materials, other research has a broader concern and addresses the development of the entire program. While many of the design and development principles are used in both product and program design, techniques often vary when one deals with large bodies of content. These studies commonly include various forms of program evaluation strategies as well as employ many typical methods found in product development research. Martin and Bramble's (1996) research is a good example. They used instructional systems design (ISD) procedures to reconfigure a traditional military training program into one delivered by interactive television. The program evaluation phase focused on instructional strategy effectiveness and the impact of the new delivery format on learner achievement. Below we will examine Sullivan, Ice, and Niedermeyer (2000), a comprehensive program evaluation effort. This research not only deals with a large body of content, but the program was implemented on a large scale for a long time period.

A Representative Program
Evaluation Study

Sullivan, Ice, and Niedermeyer's (2000) study is representative of program development research that focuses on the impact of an instructional program rather than the design and development procedures per se. Practitioners can learn a great deal from research of this type, even though instructional design (ID) processes themselves are not highlighted.

Sullivan et al. used field evaluation strategies to test a comprehensive K–12 energy education curriculum that was the product of a long-term instructional development and implementation project. The project had been ongoing for 20 years. The field evaluation report includes a description of the program design and the instructional materials that were developed. Implementation and revision procedures were then documented and impact data were collected using student and teacher attitude surveys and student achievement tests.

The initial field test lasted for two years and included 104 teachers and over 3,000 students from elementary and high schools across six states. Regular classroom teachers delivered the instruction and administered the knowledge pretests and posttests. They also administered attitude questionnaires at the end of the tryout unit. This served as part of the formative evaluation of the materials. After this time, full-scale implementation of the program began. Similar data were collected in the first three years of implementation.

After seven years, an external evaluator conducted a more extensive field evaluation. This included using a 119-item instrument administered by teachers to 591 students who had not used the special curriculum and to 758 students who had used one to four units of the curriculum. This survey measured general energy knowledge, as well as out-of-school energy behaviors. These evaluation data were also synthesized to produce a wide-ranging list of lessons learned about large-scale program development efforts.

Few researchers have the opportunity to follow a program for such a long period of time, as did Sullivan et al. Nonetheless, the methods used in this study can be applied to many projects, even to those that involve more limited efforts.

STRATEGIES FOR RESEARCH ON DESIGN AND DEVELOPMENT PHASES

However, not all design and development research pertains to a complete project. There is a large body of work that describes only specific phases of a design and development effort. This research demonstrates a wide variety of approaches to each phase. For example, Link and Cherow-O'Leary (1990) describe research only on the needs assessment phase that uses surveys, polls, in-school testing, and focus groups. Currently, research on design and development phases is more likely to speak to data-gathering phases of the ID process: needs assessment, and formative and summative evaluation. The literature is less robust with respect to newer types of evaluation, such as confirmative evaluation, or design phases, such as content sequencing and strategy selection.

We will examine two studies that are representative of research on the phases of design and development: the Fischer, Savenye, and Sullivan (2002) study and the Teachout, Sego, and Ford (1997/1998) study. Like Link and Cherow-O'Leary, each of these studies employs a variety of research methods and strategies. Like most research on the phases of design and development, these studies are directed toward very specific questions. Consequently, neither is likely to be seen as an exploratory study; instead, they are representative of descriptive and explanatory research.

A Representative Mixed Methods Study of Formative Evaluation

Fischer, Savenye, and Sullivan's (2002) research addresses formative evaluation and pertains to a computer-based course on an online financial and purchasing system. Typical of most formative evaluation endeavors, its basic purpose was to verify program effectiveness and identify necessary course revisions. The formative evaluation, however, was designed with concern for process-cost effectiveness, even as it assumed a comprehensive orientation.

The formative evaluation occurred in three stages in the design and development effort. These were:

- An expert review of content and user interface design during the development phase.
- One-on-one evaluations of the instruction prior to tryout.
- A full-scale tryout.

Subject matter experts, programmers, instructional designers, and trainers conducted the expert review. They were all members of the design and development team. Their suggestions served as the basis for revisions throughout the course-development process. One-on-one evaluations were conducted with three employees with special knowledge of the subject matter and typical user needs. These evaluations resulted in further course revisions.

The full-scale tryout of the course involved 78 typical trainees meeting in groups of eight to eleven over a two-month period. One instructor conducted all tryout training, and this person had been a member of the ID team. All tryout data was collected online. This included (a) posttest knowledge scores pertaining to course content, (b) posttest performance scores, (c) user attitude-survey scores, (d) learning paths, and (e) time-on-page data. Analyses of these data led to still further changes in the course.

Fischer et al. utilized both qualitative (expert review and in-depth interviews during the one-on-one evaluations) and quantitative (surveys, tests, work data) measures. The study provides a model for how one approach to formative evaluation as well as a discussion of lessons learned with respect to the cost and time allocated to such activities.

A Representative Multiple Quantitative Methods Study of Integrated Evaluation

Teachout, Sego, and Ford's (1997/1998) research describes a method for combining three different approaches to summative evaluation of instruction: measuring training effectiveness, training efficiency, and transfer of training. First, Teachout et al. had to operationally define each variable and identify their indicators. Training effectiveness was measured through supervisory ratings of on-the-job performance of the task that had been taught. These data were collected eight months after training. Transfer was measured using self-reports of the number of times a trainee performed each trained task on the job. Training efficiency related to the amount of time that had been allocated to each task taught in the course. Each task was classified as either over-training, under-training, or as a training match. This was determined by transforming learning difficulty ratings and training-time measurements into standard scores with a mean of 0 and a standard deviation of 1.

These evaluations measures were applied to an 18-week U.S. Air Force training course that covered 99 tasks. There were 182 participants. The training manager, the course developers, and the instructors completed course-content analyses. One hundred eighty-two supervisors of the training graduates provided the performance ratings.

The uniqueness of this approach to evaluation is not simply the distinctive measures, but the manner in which the data are combined. The training efficiency, effectiveness, and transfer data are linked and their relationships highlighted in tables. In summary, the researchers found that "tasks that are overtrained are performed more frequently on the job than the other tasks and are performed to a higher level of effectiveness" (p. 177). These evaluation results provide insights that can be easily directed toward further course development; in a manner, it is similar to using formative evaluation data.

Teachout et al. were engaged in exploratory design and development research. Their methodologies are all quantitative—primarily survey strategies combined with quantitative analyses of course content and an array of statistical techniques.

STRATEGIES FOR RESEARCH ON TOOL DEVELOPMENT AND USE

Recently, some design and development researchers have been concentrating on studying the development and use of tools, rather than on products or programs. These tools either make design and development itself easier, or support the teaching/learning process. Not surprisingly, the bulk of these have been computer-based tools, and research has been directed toward automating design and development through their use. For example, Gettman, McNelly, and Muraida (1999) describe the Guided Approach to Instructional Design Advising (GAIDA), a program that provides online direction to novice designers. Mooij's (2002) research, focusing on an instructional management system for early education, is also an example of a tool development study.

Tool development research uses many of the same methods and strategies as does product development research. It relies greatly on case study methodologies and evaluation techniques. We will examine two representative tool studies. Chou and Sun (1996) exemplifies research on the development of an instructional support system and Nieveen and van den Akker's (1999) study reports on the design and evaluation of a computer system that supports designers.

A Representative Tool Development Case Study

Chou and Sun's (1996) study describes the development of CORAL, a network-based computer-assisted learning system designed to encourage and support communication among distance learning students in Taiwan. This case study follows the phases of the traditional ISD model: analysis and design, development, and evaluation. A team that included faculty and students, both representing network engineers and educators, conducted the project.

During the analysis and design phase, data were collected from 42 representative learners covering (a) demographic profiles; (b) past experiences with cooperative learning; (c) computer network knowledge; and (d) cognitive, behavioral, and attitudinal characteristics. These data were critical to the eventual design of the user-centered tool that focused upon a scenario of a student engaged in a learning task.

During the development phase, "a working prototype course consisting of 100 instructional nodes was created so that the system, course, and interface could be more easily visualized and evaluated" (Chou & Sun, 1996, p. 76). The prototype course and communication system were tried out during this phase and the target students' navigation paths were collected and analyzed. The system included built-in recording and tracking functions that allowed researchers to gather and analyze information on student navigation paths.

The formative evaluation phase was primarily intended to examine the usability of the interface and the effectiveness of the course as it was conducted using the communication tool. This had two phases. The first phase involved expert review and the second consisted of a learner tryout. The expert review included a content analysis by a subject matter expert (SME), and interface analyses by two experts with specialization in interface design and two experts in computer networks and usability.

The usability review centered around 10 heuristics derived from a review of the literature. The same 42 students who participated in the learner analysis then completed the distance learning course using the CORAL tool. A group project was embedded in this instruction to specifically test the extent to which CORAL facilitated interpersonal communication and cooperative work. Student data included achievement tests as well as attitude questionnaires. In addition, there were observations of selected students during their learning experiences; these were followed by in-depth interviews to complete the usability testing.

As is typical of most formative evaluations, this one led to a series of revisions in the communication system, the course, and the interface. However, the ISD procedures followed in this case also allow designers to determine the relationships between the system attributes and student behaviors.

This case study documents an ISD process that is intertwined with a variety of research methods. Chou and Sun document the use of surveys, literature reviews, expert reviews, field observations, and in-depth interviews. The bulk of these methods were qualitative. However, the case as a whole included elements of exploratory (e.g., the literature reviews and field observations), descriptive (e.g., expert reviews and in-depth interviews), and explanatory (e.g., analyses of system attributes and student behaviors) research.

A Representative Tool Use Study

Nieveen and van den Akker's (1999) tool research focuses on a computer system that serves as a performance support tool for designers during the formative evaluation phase of an ID project. This is part of a series of studies on Computer Assisted Curriculum Analysis, Design and Evaluation (CASCADE). This particular study concentrates on the use of the tool; it seeks to assess not only the tool's effectiveness, but its practicality as well. This research had two components: (a) a workshop that involved a simulation of only one part of the formative evaluation process designed to determine the practicality of the tool, and (b) a full-scale tryout of the tool in a natural work setting.

Sixty-five designer/developers participated in one of four presentations of the four-hour workshop. A pre-session survey was used to identify participant background characteristics. The participating designers varied in terms of experience and expertise. The first two hours were devoted to training in the use of the formative evaluation tool. Because the researchers were interested in the extent to which designers could use the tool independently, this training was limited to explanations of CASCADE's support components and the user interface; no conceptual background information was provided. Participating designers then had one hour to use the tool to develop a formative evaluation plan for an actual case from their own work. The system was able to save participant actions and time-on-screen data. The workshop leader and assistant noted any comments and support that they provided to designers during the exercise. The contents of the evaluation plans constructed during the workshop were collected for analysis, and a post-workshop questionnaire was used to gather perceptions of practicality and other reactions to the tool. The results of this study confirmed that the tool was "fairly practical" (p. 90), but "not fully self-explanatory" (p. 91).

The second part of the assessment involved a tryout with four ID projects currently underway in two different work settings. Three of the designers were experienced; one was a novice. Their selection was not random, but was based upon their willingness to cooperate and whether the timing of the formative evaluation phase in their projects coincided with the timing of the research. Data collected included:

- Two or three interviews per designer after completion of significant parts of the formative evaluation task.
- Documentation of the evaluation activities completed (evaluation plan, instruments, final report, log book of activities).

Using a synthesis of the data collected, a detailed report of each tryout project was written. Summaries of these project reports were written. Participating designers then reviewed these summaries and recommended minor changes. The findings of this research led to changes in the tool, confirmation of the assumption that the tool was appropriate for both novice and experienced designers, and an identification of the constraints of daily practice that impacted the tool's use and effectiveness.

Like many other examples of design and development research, this tool-use study used a mixed methods design. In Phase 1 the methods employed were survey research techniques and content analysis. In Phase 2 the methods were in-depth interview and content analysis. This study was primarily descriptive, although some explanatory tasks were undertaken.

A SUMMARY OF PRODUCT
AND TOOL RESEARCH DESIGNS

We have now analyzed seven examples of methods and strategies used in product and tool research. Hopefully, these will stimulate your thinking as you design similar studies of your own. As you think about the designs, note the many ways in which these researchers have dealt with the standard concerns of any research design: establishing validity, facilitating causal inferences, facilitating generalizations and interpretations, and anticipating and avoiding problems. Each study has its own unique way of dealing with these concerns. Table 4–1 highlights many of the ways that these concerns have been dealt with in the seven representative studies we have just examined.

In product and tool research, validity is established in large part through rigorous application of the design and development processes and of the manner in which the products or tools are implemented. Thus, activities such as needs assessments, pilot studies, frequent expert review, and careful training of tryout instructors are critical. Rigorous compliance with a particular design and

TABLE 4–1.
Representative Research Design Techniques Used in Product
and Tool Research

Research Design Concern	Type of Research	Techniques Used to Address Concern
Validity	• Product Development	• Conduct a needs assessment to determine product specifications
		• Conduct a pilot study to establish product prototype
		• Avoid sequencing effects in product use tests
		• Verify interview data with related documentation
		• Insure neutrality of try-out instructors
		• Train instructors in proper product use
		• Base product refinements on replicated testing
	• Program Development	• Field test program and evaluation procedures
		• Provide evidence of learner achievement and motivation
		• Collect usability data
	• Phases of Design & Development	• Use rubrics to score performance tests
		• Verify try-out data through consultations with participants
		• Operationally define and measure new design constructs
		• Update evaluation data to reassess needs and resource allocations
	• Tool Development & Use	• Use experts with differing areas of specialization for tool review
		• Include technicians on design team to authenticate tool construction decisions
		• Have participants verify reports of tool use
		• Select designers with varying levels of expertise to test tool
Causal Inferences	• Product Development	• Relate product design to learner achievement
	• Phases of Design & Development	• Relate product design to learner attitudes

(continued)

TABLE 4–1. (*Continued*)

Research Design Concern	Type of Research	Techniques Used to Address Concern
	• Program Development	• Relate product design to product usability • Relate design procedures to costs • Examine the interactive effects of evaluation measures • Relate program design procedures to evaluation results • Relate program design to student achievement • Relate program design to student and instructor attitudes • Relate program participation to out-of-school or work behaviors
	• Tool Development & Use	• Relate tool attributes to learner behaviors • Determine tool's practicality • Determine tool's effectiveness
Generalization and Interpretation	• Product Development	• Collect data to permit detailed descriptions of design procedures • Collect implementation data from course logbooks • Provide evidence of cost effectiveness • Try-out product in multiple situations • Make development data public to facilitate product use in other settings • Determine lessons learned
	• Program Development	• Determine long-term effects of program • Determine transfer effects of program
	• Phases of Design & Development	• View phases broadly when collecting data • Define outcomes broadly when collecting data • Interpret training effectiveness in terms of training efficiency

(*continued*)

TABLE 4–1. (*Continued*)

Research Design Concern	Type of Research	Techniques Used to Address Concern
	• Tool Development & Use	• Conduct usability analyses • Recognize "real world" constraints on tool use • Plan for tool's independent use
Anticipating Problems	• Product Development	• Conduct a pilot study to test product feasibility • Use vernacular language rather than official language in instructional materials • Test web-based prototypes on multiple browsers • Minimize assumptions of existing user knowledge
	• Program Development • Phases of Design & Development	• Collect student data via instructors • Use ID team members to conduct try-outs • Format data to facilitate training decisions
	• Tool Development & Use	• Consider cultural norms when analyzing student data • Build data collection functions into the tool

development approach, however, is not the only condition required to establish product and tool research validity. Internal and external validity of the study's dataset is also dependent upon the standard conventions espoused by Campbell and Stanley (1963).

Products and tools are deemed successful only if the research can produce data that provides evidence of noteworthy changes in learner knowledge, attitudes, and behavior. Causal effects attributed to the product may be identified using these measures. In addition, product and tool studies can determine relationships between the product's usability, practicality, cost effectiveness, and design characteristics. These conclusions are only possible, however, if the researcher collects a variety of types of data. Ideally, these data would stem from multiple design settings and the products would be usable in a number of similar instructional settings, but replication data of this type are seldom found in the literature.

Product and tool studies are often complex and can take place over a long period of time. Many things can go wrong. Only creative, detail-oriented researchers who have a good sense of the situation under study can predict these problems and take steps to avoid them. Our highlighted studies have demonstrated how this can be done.

UNIQUE PRODUCT AND TOOL
RESEARCH DESIGN CONCERNS

Throughout this chapter we have discussed design and development research methods and strategies in light of those issues that are considered when designing any piece of research. However, there are issues that tend to be more problematic for product and tool researchers than for scholars dealing with other topics. We will discuss two here:

- Avoiding biases when researchers assume participant roles.
- Recognizing the influence of work environment characteristics.

Researcher-Participant Dual Roles

In most research, it is unusual for the researcher to be a part of the observations. In ethnographic and field research, the role of the participant-observer has been recognized. Here the observer participates in the lives of the people and situations under study for an extended period of time. It is hoped that the observers will become accepted members of the community in order to understand the activities and events (Singleton & Straits, 2005). In spite of the researcher's close association with the target community, from a scientific point of view it is always clear that participant-observers are still primarily observers. "The researcher who ceases to be conscious of the observer role is said to be **going native**" (Singleton & Straits, 2005, p. 318).

In design and development research, especially in product and tool development studies, researchers often *are* the designer/developers. In other words, by design they "go native" and observe themselves. This is a far different matter than participant observation and invites the possibility of serious flaws in the data. Any time that researchers assume dual roles in a project, the study's research design must delineate specific strategies for ensuring non-biased data. Using carefully structured data-collection instruments and multiple sources of data are the most common techniques of doing this.

McKenney and van den Akker (2005) assumed the multiple roles of not only researchers and designers, but also developers, programmers, and evaluators. This was an expedient and a reasonable arrangement in their circumstances. They used the following strategies to avoid interjecting personal biases into the data set:

- Establishing procedures to segregate data and subjective inferences.
- Triangulating data by collecting data of different types, and data from different sources.
- Using different investigators to collect data.
- Conducting data analysis and interpretation with a larger group of colleagues and research assistants.

These are reasonable procedures that could also be applied in other studies in which the researcher assumes the role of the designer/developer.

Forsyth (1998) also combined the researcher and designer roles in one phase of her study, albeit on a simpler level than that of McKenney and van den Akker. To avoid biases, she controlled data through the structure of the log used for data collection at a regularly established schedule during the design and development process. The instructional product she produced, however, was also tested in terms of participant reactions. In this way, data collected from others also influenced the final conclusions.

If researchers do assume participant roles in product and tool research, it is more likely to be that of the designer, but not always. As noted earlier, Visser (1998) was also the instructor in the tryout of her product. This situation is not unusual. Once again, procedures must be established that avoid allowing the researcher to unintentionally interject biases into the dataset.

Research in a Natural Work Environment

Design and development research is by nature an applied type of research. Most studies seek to collect data from realistic design and development situations, either simulated or naturally occurring. Product and tool research is almost exclusively the study of actual design and development efforts. When studying ID processes that occur in "real world" settings, one is blessed with authenticity and cursed with a myriad of contextual factors, some of which are relevant and others that are not. Unlike model research, product and tool research tends to relate to just one project, and in turn just one context. By and large, these studies recognize the influence of their work environments through full descriptions. This is typical of case-study methodology.

In the studies we have examined in this chapter, many aspects of work settings and instructional contexts have been described. These include:

- The characteristics of the program in which the product was tried out (Visser et al., 2002).
- The characteristics and backgrounds of the learners for whom the product, program, or tool was designed (Chou & Sun, 1996; Fischer et al., 2002; Mooij, 2002).
- The characteristics and backgrounds of the designer/developers for whom the tool was designed (Nieveen & van den Akker, 1999).
- The structure of the design and development team that created the tool (Chou & Sun, 1996).
- The facilities used for product implementation (Corry et al., 1997; Fischer et al., 2002).
- Resources and procedures utilized in the distribution and implementation of the program (Sullivan et al., 2000).

In addition to including contextual variables in case studies, some product and tool studies address such factors in quantitative analyses. Typically, this occurs in a product- or program-evaluation phase. For example, Sullivan et al. (2000) measured school administrator attitudes (an organizational climate characteristic) and considered its impact on the success of the energy curriculum developed by the authors.

LOOKING AHEAD

In this chapter, we have explored design and development research focused on specific products or tools. We have provided strategies for designing these types of studies and shown how design and development researchers have addressed concerns related to validity, generalizability, and other important issues. On the next page, we offer a checklist to address concerns commonly faced by product and tool researchers. In the next chapter, we continue our examination of design and development research by focusing on methods and strategies used in studies of model development, validation, and use.

**A CHECKLIST FOR ADDRESSING
COMMON CONCERNS OF PRODUCT
AND TOOL RESEARCH DESIGN**

1. Determine if the study will be conducted while design and development activities are occurring or if retrospective data will be used.
2. Use formative, summative, and/or confirmative evaluation to address questions of product and tool impact such as the following:
   - Is the product or tool usable and practical?
   - Is the product or tool cost effective and does it provide an appropriate return on investment?
   - Does it impact attitude, learning, performance and organizational results?
3. Identify techniques that provide for objective data collection, especially if you are serving as both designer/developer and researcher.
4. Establish validity of data and the subsequent findings so that the following questions can be addressed:
   - Are the data supported by multiple sources?
   - Have all biases been avoided?
   - Have in-progress data been collected whenever possible?
   - Have design and development procedures and instruments been piloted?
5. Facilitate generalizability so that the following questions can be addressed:
   - Are the findings sustained over time?
   - Are the findings sustained across settings?
   - Are the findings sustained with varying designers/developers?
   - Can the findings be interpreted broadly?
6. Anticipate and control potential problems by addressing the following questions:
   - Have any technical barriers of product evaluation or use been removed?
   - Have unique designer/learner characteristics been accommodated?
   - Have constraints imposed by a natural work environment been accommodated?

5

Model Research:
Methods and Strategies

In the previous chapter we discussed methods and strategies for research on products and tools. In addition to these types of studies, research can focus on the development, validation, or use of a model. Some studies address more than one of these concerns. These studies are the most generalized form of design and development research. As with product and tool research, their primary goal is the production of new knowledge; in this case, the knowledge is often in the form of a new or an enhanced design model. This type of research highlights either comprehensive models or particular design techniques or processes.

In this chapter we will describe representative model research. We will examine the methodologies employed in studies of:

- Model development.
- Model validation.
- Model use.

STRATEGIES OF MODEL
DEVELOPMENT RESEARCH

In spite of the widespread use of models in the field of instructional design, there is a paucity of research on model formation. Dick's (1997) discussion of the initial formation of the influential Dick and Carey model shows model construction as a process of applying a diverse body of research and thinking of the times to the task of creating instructional products. It was a logical process of synthesis.

Today, most new ID models are constructed in a similar fashion. For example, Tessmer, McCann, and Ludvigsen's (1999) research produced and validated a model for the reassessment of the need for existing training. Similar to the construction of the Dick and Carey model, this model was developed by analyzing formative evaluation theory and research. Thus, the research technique employed was that of conducting a literature review and synthesizing the findings.

However, there is research that specifically addresses model construction procedures. We will examine two representative studies: Jones and Richey (2000) and Spector, Muraida, and Marlino (1992). In both studies the newly developed models were based upon data collected directly from designers/developers. In one study the designers were recollecting the tasks that occur in real-life design projects. In the other, data were collected during a simulated design and development task. One study used a multiple method approach, and the other used a mixed method approach.

A Representative Multiple Qualitative Methods Study

The Jones and Richey (2000) research produced a revised rapid prototyping ID model that describes designer tasks performed, the concurrent processing of those tasks, and the nature of customer involvement. Data were obtained from a natural design and development work setting. Designers and clients from two contrasting projects participated in the study. The projects varied in terms of size, product, and industry. One produced paper-based instructional materials; the other produced electronic-based materials. Both projects had been completed at the time of the research.

The designers constructed task logs in which they identified the tasks they had completed, when they were completed, and the time it took to do each job. As part of the logging process, designers reviewed extant data, including the project proposal, time sheets, design memos, prototype specifications, memos, and the final product.

Next, a structured one-hour interview was conducted with each designer to determine the impact of the rapid prototyping methodologies on the ID process and on product quality. Telephone interviews were conducted with the customer. All interviews were tape-recorded.

After coding and synthesizing the data, the researchers could see exactly which design and development tasks were performed when and by whom. The time expended on each task was determined and an ID rapid-prototyping procedural model was devised. The primary methods used in this model development research were content analysis of extant data and newly constructed diaries, and in-depth interviews.

A Representative Mixed Method Study

Spector, Muraida, and Marlino (1992) produced a cognitively oriented model for designing computer-based instruction (CBI) based upon simulated design and development activities. A key objective of the model was to describe the shifts between analytic and intuitive thinking that occurred during the ID process. The components of an input-process-output model of a CBI design task were hypothesized based upon a literature review. Data pertaining to each of these components were collected from 16 designers. Prior to the design task, participants completed a biographical profile inventory. Designers then had 30 hours to complete a specified ID task and keep a log of their observations about the development software they had been provided. In addition, external observers recorded the designers' reactions to the task and questions. Design time was tracked in the development software. When the lessons were completed, they underwent a peer review and the designers were given a structured exit interview. The materials were also available for immediate student tryout.

The initially hypothesized input-process-output model was supported by the data. In addition, relationships between designer expertise and designer use of the software were noted. The primary methods used in this model development research were survey, field observations, and a content analysis of the logs written during the design task.

STRATEGIES OF MODEL VALIDATION RESEARCH

In contrast to the gaps in the model construction literature, there is more literature focused on the systematic validation of ID models. Richey (2005) describes five different approaches to validation, including three methods of internal validation (expert review, usability documentation, and component investigation), and two methods of external validation (field evaluation and controlled testing). We will explore specific design and development studies here that employ each of these strategies.

A Representative Expert Review Study

Weston, McAlpine, and Bordonaro (1995) constructed and validated a model directed toward the formative evaluation phase of the ID process. Their model emphasized four components of data collection and revision: participants, roles, methods, and situations. Their validation procedures utilized a type of expert review. As with other types of model research using expert review, this study sought to determine if there were data to support the components of their proposed model. Many expert review studies collect data directly from persons serving as subject-matter experts. These studies often use strategies such as in-depth interviews (e.g., Cowell, 2001) or Delphi techniques (e.g., Tracey & Richey, in press). Weston et al. used a different approach, utilizing the writings of experts as a source of validation data.

Weston et al.'s expert review approach was based upon content analyses of 11 commonly cited texts in instructional design or formative evaluation. These texts were reviewed to identify descriptions of the four key components in their formative evaluation model. This first level of analysis provided a basic level of expert support for the model. These descriptive segments were then analyzed to determine the experts' support for the more detailed components of the model in question. The results of this analysis were presented in both a narrative fashion as well as a qualitative summary to show the level of support for each facet of the model components.

A Representative Usability
Documentation Study

Another way of validating an ID model is by studying the ease with which the model can be used by designers and developers. It is a type of internal model validation that is often a part of a larger design and development research project.

Usability validation studies are similar in many ways to model-use research. The distinguishing feature is that usability documentation efforts are a clear part of a model construction activity. They are usually viewed as descriptive research.

The Forsyth (1998) study is a good example of how usability documentation can be embedded into a model construction and validation effort. In this case, Forsyth constructed an ISD model that would be appropriate for community-based train-the-trainer programs. This model encompassed the development and use of needs assessment and contextual analysis instruments, specification of content, development of instruments to self-check prerequisite skills, development of instructional materials (including a participant's guide and audio-visual aids), and evaluation instruments.

The study took place in three phases. The usability documentation was included in the second phase while the designer/researcher used the model to create the train-the-trainer program. To facilitate the design and development process, a binder, divided into sections matching the various steps of the proposed model, was developed. A daily log was inserted into each section that was completed by the designer during each work session. The log provided for data recordings related to each specific activity, including date and starting time, reactions, tools and resources used, and lessons learned.

The model usability data combined with the program tryout and evaluation data provided the basis for a final model that was particularly geared to the unique constraints of community-based education. Each ID phase was finalized and described in light of the typical financial and human resources available, the nature of the service, its frequency of use, and the size of the organization that would be using the model. Thus, the ultimate model was validated in terms of the setting for which it was intended.

A Representative Investigation of Component Variables

The internal validation studies we have discussed thus far pertain to ID procedural models. However, there is a genre of research that pertains to conceptual models, models that identify critical variables and the relationships between them. This research is concerned with those factors that are critical to the teaching/learning process and should therefore be addressed in an ID model. The Quiñones, Ford, Sego, and Smith (1995/96) study is typical of this type of research.

Quiñones et al. was concerned with transfer of training and examines the relationships between individual characteristics, transfer environment characteristics, and the opportunity to perform. The participants in the research were 118 graduates of a U.S. Air Force training program and their supervisors. The design made use of basic survey methodologies.

The first survey was administered to the graduates upon the completion of their training course and while they were waiting for their work assignments. This instrument collected data on the pertinent individual characteristics (locus of control, career motivation, and a measure of the amount learned in the training course). Four months after graduation a second survey was sent to the trainees at their new bases and their supervisors. Supervisors responded to attitudinal measures (perceptions of the trainee's likeability and career potential, and the supervisors' trust in the trainee's ability). The trainees responded to items that addressed their perceptions of the support they received in their workgroup and the extent to which they performed tasks that had been in their original training (number of times the task was performed and the extent to which the trainees performed difficult and challenging tasks).

These data served as the basis for testing the hypothesized conceptual models of variable relationships using LISREL VII, a sophisticated statistical modeling technique. The results showed that individual characteristics were related to the supervisor attitudes. Moreover, supervisor attitudes and a supportive climate were also related to the opportunity to perform all of which can play an important role in training design. Here, basic survey methods were used as the basis of explanatory research, rather than their more common application in descriptive studies.

A Representative Field-Evaluation Study

Design and development models can also be validated by systematically studying the effects of the products that have been created as a result of their use. Taylor and Ellis (1991) exemplify this line of external validation research when they evaluated classroom training to determine how effective the ISD model was as applied in programs of the U.S. Navy.

Taylor and Ellis selected 100 courses that were representative of the training available for enlisted personnel. After interviews with course instructors and managers, representative one-week samples of each course were selected. Objectives, test items, and classroom presentations related to these smaller samples were evaluated using a six-step process. Previous research had established the reliability and validity of this evaluation system. This system involved a review of course documentation as well as 30-minute classroom observations.

The document-review process had five steps:

1. Classify objectives using a simplified version of Merrill's Component Display Theory (see Merrill, 1983).
2. Match objectives and test items.
3. Identify and classify course training goals in terms of expected proficiency level (data from instructor interviews).
4. Determine appropriateness of each objective.
5. Determine appropriateness and adequacy of test items.

Finally, classroom instruction was observed and evaluated in terms of the consistency and the adequacy of the presentation. These evaluations highlighted (a) the nature of the presentation in relation to the type of objective, and (b) the number of design principles that promote student learning that were evident in the instructional materials and the presentations.

When field evaluations are used for ID model validation the results are also examined in terms of their implications for confirming or altering the basic model that guided the design and development projects. Taylor and Ellis (1991) did just this. Their evaluation data identified areas in which the ISD model was not being followed in the best manner, resulting problems, and those ID procedures that are most critical to student performance.

A Representative Controlled Testing Study

Design models can also be externally validated by establishing experiments that isolate the effects of the given ID model as compared to the use of another model or approach. This is the object of controlled testing validation, a form of explanatory research. Tracey (2002) is one example of this type of validation effort.

Tracey compared the use of the Dick and Carey (1996) model with an ISD model enhanced with a consideration of multiple intelligences. This served as an external validation of the newly constructed Multiple Intelligences (MI) Design Model. She established two design teams, each with two novice design-ers. One team worked with the Dick and Carey model, and the second used the MI model. Both teams were instructed to design a two-hour, instructor-led, classroom-based, team-building course for a non-profit organization. The teams each received (a) materials regarding the organization, (b) written con-tent on team building, (c) audience, environment, and gap analysis informa-tion, and (d) an ISD model. One team received the validated MI Design Model and the other the Dick and Carey model.

All four instructional designers met as a group to assess the needs, identify the goals of the team-building training, and review the content. The teams then separated to conduct their own learner and environmental analysis based on the information given and their assigned model. Both teams worked indi-vidually to create their performance objectives based on the results of their analyses and the steps of the design model they were using. The teams recon-vened to review their objectives to ensure each met the same team-building goals, and together they wrote the posttest questions. The teams then sepa-rated again and worked simultaneously in the same building in two different offices during the remainder of the design and development process. Each group was provided with computers, an office, any desired training materials, and a desktop publisher to create the instructor guide and participant guide templates and all finished products.

The resulting programs were implemented and evaluated. Instrumentation used during the experiment included designer logs giving reactions to their tasks and the models used, learner knowledge posttests, and surveys addressing participant reactions to the instruction.

The standard experimental design issues identified by Campbell and Stanley (1963) and discussed extensively in many research-methods texts must be addressed in controlled testing validation research. Although Tracey's design setting was not a natural work environment, it was very similar. Product implementation, however, was in a natural environment. There are other approaches, though. For example, Higgins and Reiser's (1985) research involved the controlled testing of a media selection model versus individual procedures that were logically devised. This involved graduate students serving as novice designers, and took place in a classroom environment.

STRATEGIES OF MODEL USE RESEARCH

Design and development research that focuses on model use is typically characterized as being either exploratory or descriptive. Exploratory research addresses ID processes as they occur naturally and intuitively in a variety of settings. Examples include Le Maistre's (1998) study of expert formative evaluation performance and Visscher-Voerman and Gustafson's (2004) study of alternative design paradigms. Descriptive research, on the other hand, tends to concentrate on the use of a particular model, such as in Roytek's (2000) study of rapid prototyping techniques. These studies also represent the three major lines of model use research-studies of the conditions impacting model use, designer decision-making research, and designer expertise and characteristics research. Although these three studies used different research designs, the designs all tend to be more qualitative than quantitative. This is characteristic of model use research. We will now examine the methods used in each study.

A Representative Expertise Study Using Think-Aloud Strategies

Le Maistre (1998) is a study of expertise and it follows in the tradition established to a great extent by Rowland's (1992) study comparing the differences between expert and novice designers. Like Rowland's study, Le Maistre's used "think-aloud" methods.

Le Maistre's study focused on a six-page self-instructional material designed for an undergraduate course in chemistry for non-chemistry majors. Formative evaluation data were collected from subject matter experts (SMEs) and learners similar to those for whom the material was targeted. Students took a pretest, worked through the materials, and then took a posttest. While they were using the materials they were asked to comment on them; these comments were audio-taped. The SMEs reviewed the materials and identified any problems they saw. Their comments were also recorded and transcribed.

Eight practicing instructional designers who met predefined criteria were selected for participation in the study. After selection, they were interviewed to make sure that they met the selection criteria and were competent to handle the revision task. They were given the SME and learner feedback data and asked to revise the materials.

An initial analysis of these revisions prompted more specific research questions, and two of the original eight designers were selected for further study. One had the most work experience (18 years), and the other had the least (5 years). They were both proficient in using the "think-aloud" techniques. The study was then replicated. The designers were given additional formative evaluation feedback data from other studies in the research program and the context in which the material had been developed, and were once again asked to "make any revisions to the unit that seem necessary." They were asked to think aloud while making the revisions and were prompted if they were silent for more than ten seconds. Afterwards, the designers participated in a structured debriefing interview to clarify any issues and confirm basic demographic information.

The think-aloud protocols were transcribed, separated into meaningful units, and coded. After three months the segmenting and coding was checked to insure reliability. The two designer datasets were analyzed to determine the manner in which an expert designer does formative evaluation and how this differs from that of a designer with less experience.

This exploratory research examined the elements of the design process as they were occurring. While think-aloud strategies were central to the study, Le Maistre also used qualitative evaluation techniques and interviews.

A Representative Designer Decision-Making Study Using In-Depth Interviews

In-depth interviews provide another way for design and development researchers to explore the intricacies of the ID process as it actually occurs. In a fashion similar to that of using the think-aloud protocols, interviewing can provide insights into how designers solve problems. Visscher-Voerman and Gustafson (2004) approached their research with no preconceived notions of how design should be done, even though they recognized the importance of the general ISD model.

Twenty-four different designers, including those with and without formal design training, were selected according to predetermined criteria. These designers represented six different design settings. The study had two phases. In the first phase, 12 designers, two per setting, were interviewed for about one and a half hours. The first interview included discussions of the designers' backgrounds and their projects. They were asked about the strategies they had used in a recent project and were encouraged to give concrete examples, and also to explain why they worked in a given manner and why they deviated from general plans. These interviews were audio-taped and transcribed. Interview data were corroborated through an examination of related project documents. Then a report was generated based upon the interviews that covered each designer's profile, a project summary, and a project description. The report was revised after the designer reviewed and reacted to it. The revised reports, rather than the interviews, were used as the basis for the preliminary analysis.

The preliminary analysis began by labeling each design activity described using ADDIE terminology: analysis, design, development, implementation, and evaluation. Next, there was a more detailed analysis of each major activity as described by each designer. These analyses were then synthesized and interpreted in light of the literature to produce four different general design paradigms (not models), each of which represents a unique philosophical orientation.

In the second round of in-depth interviews, two designers from each setting were interviewed following the same procedures as had been previously used and data were initially analyzed in the same manner. Then all data were combined and analyzed to determine the underlying rationales for designer actions. Detailed descriptions of designer activities and their underlying paradigms resulted.

This is a comprehensive exploratory study dealing with past design work, often called "reconstructive research." It is rooted in qualitative research techniques such as in-depth interviews, document analysis, and literature review.

A Representative Qualitative Study of Conditions Impacting Model Use

Another major line of model use research explores the conditions surrounding model use. These studies can use a variety of methods. For example, Carr-Chellman, Cuyar, and Breman's (1998) investigation of user design in a health-care setting used case study methods. Hallamon (2002) studied the factors that facilitate and impede the use of task analysis. He used quantitative survey research methods, polling practitioners to identify current ID practices and the workplace conditions that impacted this practice.

Roytek's (2000) conditions study was multiple methods research utilizing a variety of qualitative research techniques, including in-depth interviews and extensive document analyses. These techniques have been used in other model research studies described here, and are frequently combined to verify data reliability in design and development research. This study was explicitly directed toward the many contextual variables (pre-project, during project, and post-project) that affect the use of a specific rapid prototyping design model.

The research took place in a private consulting firm. Two projects were selected for study based upon their superior use of rapid prototyping techniques, their accessibility, and their potential for offering a rich description of the activities involved. Data were collected from nine consulting firm team members (project leader, designers/developers, and software developers) and five client team members (project managers, training managers, and an organizational development consultant).

Audio-taped structured interviews, ranging from one to one and a half hours in length, were the principal data collection method. First, participants were asked to complete a Pre-Interview Activity Form in which they recalled the firm's rapid prototyping development model and the various prototypes associated with their given project. Participants were also provided with examples of contextual factors from the literature that served as thought-starters as they prepared to be interviewed.

A variety of project-related documents were also reviewed and served as data for the study. These documents included computer-based instructional modules, e-mail messages, and professional society presentations.

All data were reviewed to identify strategies or conditions that enhance or inhibit the use of rapid prototyping. Full quotes from the interviews were reduced to a sentence or phrase and these concise phrases became known as the "strategies/conditions/events" within this study. An analysis of these statements was undertaken to discover patterns and to generate an incident-classification scheme. Thus, the study identified contextual factors and their supporting strategies, conditions, and events that enhance or inhibit the use of the targeted ID model.

A SUMMARY OF MODEL RESEARCH DESIGNS

We have now examined in some detail 10 examples of methods and strategies used in model research. As with those examples we presented in the last chapter, these should generate unique ways your own research designs can establish validity, facilitate causal inferences, facilitate generalizations and interpretations, and anticipate problems that may occur during the course of your research. Table 5–1 highlights many of the ways that these same concerns have been dealt with in the 10 representative studies we have just examined.

TABLE 5–1.
Representative Research Design Techniques Used in Model Research

Research Design Concern	Type of Design & Development Research	Techniques Used to Address Concern
Validity	• Model Development	• Use design tasks that are realistic in scope • Use data from actual design projects • Record reactions during design process • Use extant data to verify project recollections
	• Model Validation (Internal)	• Consistently use pre-defined expert selection criteria • Collect data during design process • Provide evidence of ease of designer use • Provide design & development time data
	• Model Validation (External)	• Provide evidence of learner achievement • Provide evidence of program implementation • Base evaluation system on established theory • Account for the effects of designer expertise • Account for the effects of design & development time • Account for the effects of resources available • Identify product effects
	• Model Use	• Consistently use pre-defined project, course, and/or designer selection criteria • Use multiple data sets and triangulate data • Provide structured memory prompts • Determine reliability of coding and evaluation systems • Have designers verify accuracy of interpretations
Causal Inferences	• Model Development	• Relate design behaviors to product impact

(continued)

TABLE 5–1. (*Continued*)

Research Design Concern	Type of Design & Development Research	Techniques Used to Address Concern
	• Model Validation (Internal)	• Use experts' publications as a substitute for direct interviews of them
	• Model Validation (External)	• Predict training effects from learner and contextual characteristics
		• Relate model use to training outcomes
		• Relate model use to product characteristics
	• Model Use	• Relate design activities to client satisfaction
		• Relate design activities to ISD model
		• Relate design activities to philosophical orientations
Generalization and Interpretation	• Model Development • Model Validation (Internal & External)	• Collect data from natural work settings • Collect design context data • Determine lessons learned
	• Model Validation (Internal)	• Interpret narrative descriptions broadly
	• Model Validation (External)	• Validate models in terms of use context
		• Determine necessary ID practice revisions
	• Model Use	• Account for setting effects
Anticipating Problems	• Model Development	• Audio-record and transcribe interviews
	• Model Validation (Internal & External) • Model Use	• Use instruments tested in previous research
	• Model Validation (Internal) • Model Validation (External) • Model Use	• Insure correct model use by documenting the procedures advocated in the model • Use instructors to identify critical course/program segments • Verify that selected participants actually do meet criteria • Provide prompts for non-responsive participants

Establishing validity is accomplished to a great extent by gathering as many types of data as possible (e.g., time data, paper documentation, achievement data) and making efforts to have these data as realistic as possible (e.g., reasonable task scope, using actual or simulated design tasks). In addition, extraneous variables (e.g., resources, designer expertise) are controlled or accounted for.

These model research studies can attribute the effects of a given project to the model itself by examining a variety of outcomes (e.g., the products produced, client satisfaction, learner outcomes). However, these effects are also explained in terms of other contributing factors (e.g., designer behaviors, philosophical orientation). Generalization and interpretations of these effects can be made to a great extent by examining the role of context (design, learning, and performance).

Research design strategies that are devised to counteract obstacles and problems that may arise during the research are, by and large, idiosyncratic to individual studies. However, there are general techniques that can be used to maintain data accuracy (e.g., audio-taping interviews, relying on previously verified instrumentation, using instructors and other authority figures to collect data).

UNIQUE MODEL RESEARCH DESIGN CONCERNS

As with product and tool research, there are issues that can be especially problematic for design and development researchers involved in model studies. We will discuss three here:

- Insuring the integrity of recall data.
- Accommodating the demands of multiple natural work environments.
- Dealing with a wide range of participant characteristics.

Working with Recall Data

The research studies described in this chapter show many examples of data being collected while the design and development project is underway. This is always the preferred approach, but it is not always possible, especially if one is dealing with the time constraints of real projects occurring in natural work settings. The dangers of using recall data are obvious: people may forget project details. When it is necessary to use recall data, there should be provisions for (a) using systematic procedures to prompt and stimulate participants' memories, and (b) verifying the data that is provided. There are many techniques for accomplishing these goals, and in turn ensuring the accuracy of your data. Table 5–1 highlights some strategies that were used in our sample model studies to ensure the accuracy of recall data. These strategies include

- Having participants construct project task logs and using extant data to verify these project recollections (Jones & Richey, 2000).
- Providing participants with examples from the literature in a similar category as the desired response to serve as a memory prompt (Roytek, 2000).
- Requiring participants to complete a Pre-Interview Activity Form to stimulate recall (Roytek, 2000).
- Allowing participants to verify the accuracy of their reports (Visscher-Voerman & Gustafson, 2004).

Once again, research designs that provide for multiple sources of data help ensure the reliability of a dataset.

Research in Multiple Natural Work Environments

Edmonds, Branch, and Mukherjee (1994) posit that the success of an ID model is dependent upon the extent to which there is a match between the application context and the context for which the model was originally intended. This assumption underlies the vast majority of model research. It becomes especially critical in model research since many studies deal not only with contextual issues, but also with design and development efforts that can span multiple work settings and projects. As you might expect, this can pose research design dilemmas.

Design and development contexts vary in terms of available resources and facilities, as well as the climate and emphases imposed by factors such as the organization's mission and leadership style. They also vary in terms of the characteristics of the learning and performance environments in which the subsequent instruction is implemented. Model research that addresses multiple projects especially needs to accommodate these many factors in their research designs. Contextual factors that typically impact model research pertain to:

- Project characteristics.
- Project resources and constraints.
- Organizational climate (design climate and user climate).

Each research environment must be analyzed so that the pertinent factors of that particular setting can be identified. Once identified, these workplace elements are typically accommodated in one of two ways: either through control or measurement. Many of our sample studies not only highlight these factors, but also demonstrate how they can be accommodated.

There are a variety of project characteristics that have been considered in design and development research. Projects may be selected for study in a manner that facilitates data analysis in terms of project differences. For example, in a given study, projects examined may vary in terms of delivery system (e.g., Jones & Richey, 2000) or setting (e.g., Visscher-Voerman & Gustafson, 2004, Taylor & Ellis, 1991). Another approach is to collect data on resources available to the designer (e.g., Forsyth, 1998) or constraints imposed by the organization or the project (e.g., Phillips, 2000) and include this information in your analyses.

Finally, many studies consider the impact of organizational climate factors on not only the design and development processes, but upon instruction and on-the-job performance. Quiñones et al. (1995/96) built elements such as supervisor attitudes and learner career motivation into their transfer of training model.

All of these studies have been designed so that one can determine the impact of the many factors that exist in the natural workplace, factors that are eliminated in most laboratory research. The research designs provide for a data-rich study and give design and development researchers the opportunity to draw conclusions based upon a dataset that is not only realistic, but also isolated from irrelevant details as much as possible.

Distinguishing Participant Characteristics

Design and development research is likely to have a larger number of key participants than there are in other types of research. Moreover, these participants are likely to vary widely in a number of important characteristics. This has posed research design problems, especially with respect to model research. How do you describe and differentiate among the various participants? How do you determine the impact their attributes have on the ID effort? Typical concerns of this type relate to the diverse backgrounds and characteristics of:

- Designers/developers.
- Clients.

The effects of designer expertise have been examined in many model studies, including Perez and Emery (1995) and Saroyan (1993), as well as the Rowland (1992) and Weston et al. (1995) studies that have been discussed above. The differences between the habits of expert and novice designers have proved to be critical. However, there are other important designer characteristics that also appear to influence how design and development processes are carried out. For example, Chase (2003) isolated designer gender effects and Hallamon (2002) found age effects. Shellnut (1999) considered the impact of designer background and attitudes toward motivation on the designers' use of motivation design techniques. In each of these studies the designer characteristics in question served as major variables of the research; measurements were explicitly made and the data analyzed in relation to project outcomes.

Client characteristics (including factors such as amount of experience with the ID processes, knowledge of the training field, and level of subject matter expertise) are also important parts of some design and development research. In Jones and Richey (2000), clients' previous experience with rapid prototyping design and development techniques was important to their consideration of the impact of client involvement in the projects being studied. In Carr-Chellman et al.'s (1998) case study, the professional backgrounds of clients on their user task force were described in detail.

In design and development research, perhaps even more than with other types of research, researchers need to be knowledgeable about the environments in which projects occur. Only with these understandings can one create research designs that accommodate the many factors that will influence the validity of the study's conclusions.

LOOKING AHEAD

This chapter has focused on model development, model validation, and model use research. We gave many examples of this type of design and development research and provided methods and strategies for planning these studies. On the next page, we offer a checklist to address common concerns faced in studies of models.

At this point in design and development research, you should be totally immersed in planning your study. Many decisions about method and strategy have been addressed. You not only know precisely what you will be studying, but in general you know how you will organize the research. In the next chapter, we will zero in on even more specifics of the project—namely, who will be involved? What setting will you study? How will you select participants from that setting? How will you get their consent to be involved in your study? How will you protect them from any repercussions that might occur as a result of their involvement?

A CHECKLIST FOR ADDRESSING COMMON
CONCERNS OF MODEL RESEARCH DESIGN

1. Determine if the study will examine the development, validation and/or use of a model.
2. Determine if the study will pertain to an actual or simulated design project.
3. Establish validity of data and the subsequent findings by addressing the following questions:
   - Are design/development tasks realistic in scope?
   - Have criteria governing the selection of key components of the study been predefined?
   - Have multiple data sets be used to triangulate data?
   - Have in-progress data been collected whenever possible?
   - Have techniques been established to facilitate the collection of accurate and complete retrospective data?
4. Use strategies to facilitate comparison of key aspects of design/development processes so that questions such as the following can be addressed:
   - What is the impact of design/development activities?
   - What is the relationship between context and model impact?
   - What is the relationship between participants and model impact?
   - What is the relationship between design/development activities and client satisfaction?
5. Facilitate generalizability so that the following questions can be addressed:
   - Are the findings sustained across settings and participant groups?
   - Are sufficient data collected to obtain an accurate picture of the design/development context?
6. Anticipate and control potential problems by addressing the following questions:
   - Have constraints imposed by multiple natural work settings been accommodated?
   - Have extraneous variables been controlled or accounted for?

6

Selecting Participants and Settings

At this point in the design and development research process, you have identified an important problem to study, formulated research questions related to a product, tool or model, and designed the study so you can make valid and generalizable conclusions. Now it's time to select who will participate in your research project and determine where the study will be conducted. In this chapter we will address issues related to selecting participants and settings for a study on design and development. Specifically, we will focus on:

- Selecting the setting.
- Selecting the participants.
- Examples of participants and settings from the design and development literature.
- Ethical considerations for protecting participants.
- Other participant and setting issues.

SELECTING THE SETTING OF THE STUDY

Design and development research is typically context-bound, and the nature of the conditions in which people work is typically critical. Consequently, we are going to place nearly as much emphasis on the *setting* of the study as we will on the people participating in the study.

Types of Settings and Their Characteristics

The range of general settings in which education and training takes place today is broad—and growing. The traditional view of education as only being formal courses and programs in schools and colleges is obsolete. ID applications are now made extensively in business and industrial settings, healthcare organizations, and community and government agencies. Within each of these general environments, there are many more specific types of settings as shown in Table 6–1.

Each of these different settings is set apart from the others by a particular culture and set of conditions that can have a profound impact on the design and development activities occurring there. Clearly, varying levels of material resources shapes the work being done; however, other parts of an organizational climate may have as great, or perhaps even a greater, impact on design and development. Levels of support, reward systems, organizational values—all have far-reaching effects. Many of these factors are shown in Table 6–2.

TABLE 6–1.
Settings of Design and Development Applications

General Setting	Specific Setting
Schools	Pre-School
	Grades K–12
	Higher Education
	Vocational/Trade
Business/Industry	Manufacturing
	Service, Private/Professional
	Trade & Transportation
Health Care	Hospitals
	Clinics, Private Offices
	Health Agencies
Community	Adult/Continuing Education
	Social Services Organizations
	Mass Media Organizations
Government	Military
	Local, State, National

TABLE 6–2.
Setting Elements that Impact Design and Development Research

General Element	Specific Element
Physical Materials	Resources
	Equipment
	Facilities
Organizational Climate	Organizational Goals & Values
	Organization Size
	Reward System
	Levels of Support
	Leadership Style
	Group Code
External Influences	Government Influence
	External Image/Reputation
	Market Potential
	Competition Level
	Economy
Member Characteristics	Leadership
	Middle Management
	Employees

When you select a setting for your research, or when you select people to participate in your research who come from a particular work setting, you are shaping and providing further structure to your research design. You are providing the context in which your research questions will be answered. The setting typically houses the problems on which your research is focused. The setting is filled with elements that can ultimately account for the findings of your research. Setting is critical!

Matching Settings to Research Questions

The researcher's most crucial decision with respect to setting is whether a particular setting includes the conditions and elements that are spoken to in one's research questions. Does the problem exist to which your questions relate? Are all of the various aspects of the situation that you want to study readily identifiable in this setting?

One design and development researcher, for example, was preparing to study the manner in which a particular type of performance measurement system was utilized in nonprofit organizations. The research design was completed. The research questions were constructed. The next step was to locate appropriate settings for the study. She had also built setting characteristics into her design. Various types of nonprofit organizations were to be selected (e.g., health care organizations, government organizations, charity organizations). The only difficulty was that it became impossible to find settings that used the targeted process. Therefore, either the design had to be changed, or the setting search expanded. It was a show-stopper.

Practical Issues in Setting Selection

Even if a setting can be found that perfectly matches one's research questions, there are other important issues to consider. Feasibility is an important consideration that should be addressed when selecting participants and settings for a design and development study. It is defined as the extent to which the study can be done practically and successfully. Related to feasibility are the resources available to the researcher. For example, without support from a company or organization, a researcher who wants to examine how summative evaluation is conducted by expert designers from several different cultures is likely to have limited resources to conduct his or her study.

Another practical issue relates to access provided by the organization. Lack of access to participants in a research setting can prohibit a design and development study from being conducted. A well-designed study on an important topic will never leave the drawing board without access to the individuals and organizations that are the target of the study. In 2001, one of the authors of this book planned a performance analysis to examine how airline gate agents used an innovative technology tool designed to answer customer's questions. Even though the setting had been selected and the airline had committed to the study, access to airport personnel and their workplace was severely limited after September 11. Thus the research plan was never implemented.

Finally, there is the issue of organizational proprietary rights. Many organizations, especially for-profit businesses, claim exclusive rights to the products they sell and the services they provide. These proprietary rights often extend to the products developed by instructional designers (Armstrong, 2003). When selecting settings for design and development research, it is important to consider whether the organization you plan to study will give you access to important data and grant permission to publish results beyond internal company documents. Furthermore, it is not uncommon for a senior-level manager to want to approve a research report prior to its publication.

For example, one of us recently taught a class where a group of graduate students investigated why training developers in a particular organization were having difficulty moving their courses from face-to-face to online settings. To gain entry to the organization, an associate dean was required to sign a statement of confidentiality. This statement made it very clear that the organization had propriety rights to all data obtained during the investigation. After the study was completed, one of the students (who worked for the organization) got permission from his manager to present the results at a professional conference (Klein et al., 2003). Without this permission, the "lesson learned" from the study would not have been offered to the broader community of scholars.

SELECTING THE PARTICIPANTS OF THE STUDY

Participants involved in design and development research may or may not be selected because of their association with a particular organization; however, they are most always selected because of their particular role in the design and development process. Here we will examine the kinds of participants that are typically selected for these studies and the various methods researchers use to identify them.

Types of Participants

Even though persons in a given role can participate in many disparate design and development research projects, different participant patterns are seen in product and tool studies, as well as model studies. Studies documenting and analyzing the development of an instructional product would obviously include those persons involved in designing the actual product—designers, developers, perhaps clients and perhaps evaluators. At times, the design team as a whole participates in such research. Studies of the impact of an innovative product or tool would include those who are affected by its use—clients, learners, instructors, and perhaps supervisors. Participants in model development and model use studies often parallel those in product development and use. Model validation studies can include persons in all of these roles. A list of the common participants in design and development research is shown in Table 6–3.

Participants in design and development research tend to focus on (not surprisingly) designers and developers, rather than learners and instructors. This is a key distinction between design and development research and traditional teaching-learning research. Even so, there are a wide variety of people serving in many roles that play critical parts of design and development research.

What is rather unique to design and development studies are the non-human entities that serve as research participants. For example, it is not unusual for the project itself to serve as a type of participant. Projects may be directed toward products that have either short-term or long-term implementation plans; the products may vary in terms of delivery system employed; they may vary in terms of content. Projects are selected for participation in a study in terms of their major sources of variance. The project then becomes the key

TABLE 6–3.
Common Participants in Design and Development Studies

Type of Research	Project Emphasis	Type of Participant
Product & Tool Research	Product Design & Development (Comprehensive & Phases)	Designers, Developers, Clients, Subject Matter Experts, Evaluators, Learners, Instructors, Organizations
Product & Tool Research	Tool Development & Use	Designers, Developers, Clients, Evaluators, Users
Model Research	Model Development	Designers, Developers, Evaluators, Researchers & Theorists
Model Research	Model Validation	Designers, Developers, Evaluators, Clients, Learners, Instructors, Organizations
Model Research	Model Use	Designers, Developers, Evaluators, Clients

unit of analysis in the study—that is, projects are the focus of the study and as such participating projects are compared one to the other.

In some design and development studies, the participants are organizations themselves. Types of organizations may be selected to provide a systematic distribution of setting constraints within a particular study. In this way, environmental effects may be identified. The organization's size in terms of personnel or budget, its focus, its philosophy—all can be factors in selecting particular organizations to participate in a study.

Sampling Participants

Like other educational researchers, a scholar who conducts design and development research typically selects a sample of participants from a population of interest following prescribed quantitative or qualitative sampling techniques.[1] These techniques help establish the validity of the ultimate conclusions and facilitate the generalizabilty and interpretations that can be made. Following, we discuss two sampling issues.

---

[1]Readers who want to know more about sampling techniques in quantitative and qualitative research should read *Educational Research: An Introduction* by Gall, Gall and Borg (2003) or one of the many other books that address the topic.

Random sampling. The selection of participants and settings for a study depends to a great extent upon whether the research has a quantitative or a qualitative orientation. Quantitative researchers typically employ *random sampling* techniques so that their study will meet the condition of population validity (Bracht & Glass, 1968). This occurs when the results obtained from a sample of participants can be generalized to the larger population they represent. Random sampling means that every accessible member of a population has an equal chance of being selected to participate in the study. The use of random sampling is at the cornerstone of experimental and quasi-experimental research designs. It is of special concern to survey researchers who wish to generalize their findings beyond those who complete their questionnaires, and survey components of a design and development study are the most likely targets for random sampling. However, as Leedy (1985) cautioned, "The results of a survey are no more trustworthy than the quality of the population or the representativeness of the sample" (p. 144).

There are certain conditions, however, that must be met in order to make a random selection of participants for a study. First, the population must be identifiable. What is the population's exact size? Who exactly is included in the population? Researchers don't always have access to such information, but they do make efforts to find smaller more identifiable groups that they use to represent the larger population. For example, it's probably impossible to identify the entire population of trainers throughout the world, but it may be possible to obtain the list of members of the American Society of Training and Development. These lists can then serve as the identified population. Such tactics are not totally devoid of difficulties given the characteristics that distinguish organization members from non-joiners, but often serve as a reasonable substitute.

Purposeful sampling. Researchers who conduct qualitative studies typically employ a technique called *purposeful (or criterion) sampling* to select participants, and settings as well. The participants are selected to match the criteria of the study (Rudestam & Newton, 2001). According to Patton (2001), the goal of purposeful sampling is to select cases that are "information-rich" to develop an understanding of the situation being studied.[2] This can be accomplished in a number of ways. You can select a "typical case," such as when a field test of an instructional program is conducted in classrooms representative of a target population (Sullivan et al., 2000), or by examining an "intense case," such as the study of expert designers using a particular model or technique (Jones & Richey, 2000).

---

[2] See Patton (2001) for a list of 15 techniques that can be used in purposeful sampling.

For qualitative researchers, the participants selected for a study are viewed as the "experiential experts of the phenomenon being studied" (Rudestam & Newton, 2001, p. 92). Typically, there is a relatively small number of people selected for this role, but unlike random sampling from a defined population, it is difficult to specify what constitutes an appropriate number. Often researchers will sample and collect data until no new information is discovered. Brewer and Hunter (2006) describe the sampling dilemma of qualitative researchers. Do you put your resources into studying a few cases in great detail and thereby risking the ability to convincingly make generalizations, or do you learn less about a larger but more systematically selected group?

Using a sample of convenience.   A distinction, however, should be made between purposeful sampling, where participants and settings are selected based on established research questions, and convenience sampling, where cases are selected because they are available and easy to study. Many examples of convenience sampling can be found in the design and development literature. Though common, this approach should be avoided whenever possible, as it can lead to biased interpretations. Convenience sampling, however, is not the same as the systematic selection of an appropriate setting that allows access to participants.

Another sampling pitfall to avoid is volunteerism; this occurs when researchers simply send out a call for volunteers to participate in their studies and select whoever responds (Patten, 2004). One solution to sampling problems is to use *purposeful random* sampling techniques, selecting a case at random from an array of many potential ones; this can help the researcher avoid sample selection bias and gain credibility (Gall et al., 2003).

PARTICIPANT AND SETTING
SOLUTIONS FROM THE DESIGN
AND DEVELOPMENT LITERATURE

Design and development research can be conducted in a myriad of settings such as pre K–12 schools, universities, businesses and industries, health care organizations, government, and the military. Furthermore, researchers can collect data from participants from many different roles, including designers, developers, evaluators, instructors, mangers, experts, learners, and clients. At times, data are collected from participants who are examined in isolation from their work settings. Below we provide examples of participants and settings that have been examined in actual studies of design and development and brief analyses of techniques that have been employed.

Participants and Settings in Product and Tool Research

Product and tool studies, for the most part, are all intimately involved with the setting in which the projects occur. Typically, the setting influences the design and development processes as much as the persons doing the work and the users of the products. Context is critical to process.

Ottevanger—Curriculum Design and Implementation in African Schools. Ottevanger (2001) conducted dissertation research on the analysis, design, implementation, and evaluation of science curriculum materials in Namibia, a country located in southern Africa. The project was conducted in several phases; prototypes of the materials were developed and evaluated at each phase. Participants included subject-matter experts who worked for the Namibian Ministry of Education and Culture, authors of science textbooks, classroom teachers and their students.

This study shows how design and development research can be used to study systematic design principles in an international setting. The setting is a critical element of the research. Moreover, setting is approached generally (i.e., the Namibian education system) as well as specifically (e.g., individual schools in the system). This study is also a good example of having different participants for different phases of the research. Purposeful sampling techniques are used throughout the various phases of the study.

Link and Cherow-O'Leary—Research and Development of Print Materials for Children and their Parents. Link and Cherow-O'Leary (1990) described how the Children's Television Workshop (CTW) uses research and evaluation to examine the appeal and suitability of print based materials that "spin-off" of popular television shows such as Sesame Street. Participants included preschool and elementary school teachers and children in day care centers, summer camps, and after-school programs. Parents and elementary school teachers examined prototypes of materials and participated in interviews and focus groups to determine the appropriateness of materials for children and adults.

Here the setting is not as critical as it was in the Ottevanger research. This is unusual for product and tool research. The characteristics and attitudes of the various participants are far more important in the study. These participants are good examples of the participant in the role of an experienced expert on the topic at hand. The focus groups of children, parents, and teachers were all formed using purposeful techniques.

Koszalka—Design in a Synchronous Distance Education Setting. Koszalka (2001) described the design and formative evaluation of a synchronous, distance education lesson that included real-time interaction between students and an expert. Participants were an online facilitator (who was a content expert) and employees of NASA, who were identified through training administrators at several government offices.

The participants in this study were all product users—the facilitator who led the instruction and the NASA employees who were learners. In this research, there was no sampling at all; instead, the entire population was included. It is a population, however, with unique characteristics because of the setting in which the instruction occurs.

Gettman, McNelly, and Muraida—A Study of Novice Designers in a Military Setting. Gettman et al. (1999) described the development and evaluation of an electronic performance support system (EPSS) to increase ID expertise in novice instructional designers. The Guided Approach to Instructional Design Advising (GAIDA) tool was developed to support subject-matter experts design lessons using Gagne's (1985) nine events of instruction. Participants were U.S. Air Force training personnel who used the tool to design instruction.

The formative evaluation of this tool, however, was replicated in various settings and with different participants. Not only was the tool used with U.S. Air Force personnel, but also with graduate students in a traditional academic setting.

Participants and Settings in Model Research

Beauchamp—Validating an ID model with Educators Working in Alternative School Settings. Beauchamp (1991) developed and validated a model that integrated components of instructional systems design with affective variables. Participants were teachers and school administrators who were members of a statewide organization of alternative educators; they completed a survey on the degree to which components of the model were used in their instructional design practices.

Other settings besides alternative schools could have been selected for this study, but this was appropriate because of alternative educator's typical interest in affective concerns. Participants were selected by using random sampling techniques. This was possible since a list of the professional organization's members provided an accurate description of the population as a whole. (Krejcie and Morgan, 1970, provided the rationale for the sample size.) The particular participants once identified were also described in terms of the communities they represented and their schools. Therefore, in effect, the communities and schools also became types of organizational participants.

Fox and Klein—Performance Improvement Competencies for Instructional Design and Technology Students. Fox and Klein (2003) reported the results of a study conducted to determine what knowledge and skills instructional design and technology (IDT) graduate students should acquire in the area of human performance technology (HPT). Participants were faculty members from several leading IDT academic programs and practitioners who were members of either the American Society for Training and Development or the International Society for Performance Improvement. The findings of the study were used to develop goals and objectives for a graduate-level course on HPT.

Two sampling techniques were used in this research. The sampling of IDT graduate faculty was a type of purposeful sampling. Only faculty from universities with IDT programs that emphasized performance improvement were contacted. Practitioners were selected from local professional groups, accessible populations. Unlike the Beauchamp study, this group did not have a predefined population, since a self-subscribed Listserv was used to contact potential participants, and the total number of subscribers was unknown.

Carliner—Designer Decision-Making in an Informal Learning Setting. Carliner (1998) conducted a qualitative study to examine how ID is practiced in the design of museum exhibits. Participants were members of "core design teams" responsible for the design, development, and installation of exhibits in three museums focused on science, technology, or history. The study shows how design and development research can be used in informal learning settings.

In this research, the museum setting was critical. The study was important because of the unique setting. The particular museums, however, were selected with a purpose. Only museums that dealt with a broad array of technical content were considered. Then one exhibit from each museum was selected for study. The design team connected to each target exhibit became the human participants; however, their selection was dependent upon the organizational and project participant decisions made first.

Twitchell, Holton, and Trott—Evaluation Practices of Technical Trainers in Business and Industry Settings. Twitchell et al. (2000) surveyed technical trainers in the United States to determine the degree to which they utilized accepted evaluation practices. The researchers excluded individuals who worked in schools, government agencies, and consulting firms. This allowed them to obtain a purposeful random sample of trainers from business and industry who were members of the American Society for Training and Development (ASTD).

While this study's population was huge (all U.S. businesses that provide technical training), the accessible population was much smaller (the 2,569 organizations with members of one division of ASTD). This group had a definable membership, and it was then possible to select a random sample of participants for the research. (Cochran, 1977, provided the rationale for their sample size.) Even though trainers provided the data in this study, the organizations for which they worked were the real target of interest.

Carr-Chellman, Cuyar, and Breman—User Design in a Health Care Setting. Carr-Chellman et al. (1998) investigated how user-design principles were employed by a team of heath care professionals charged with developing an information technology system. Participants included a sample of employees representing various stakeholders including nurses, therapists, office managers, accountants, secretaries, and corporate executives. This case study shows how design practices typically employed by software developers can be used by other types of professionals.

As in the Carliner (1998) study, the setting is a major focus of this study. The finding of this research cannot be separated from the intricacies of the health care arena. There are a large number of participants in this study, all of whom were selected because they were associated with the target design and development project. As such, the researchers used a type of purposeful sampling. The sampling techniques could also be considered stratified in that all major employee groups were included as study participants.

ETHICAL CONSIDERATIONS FOR THE PROTECTION OF PARTICIPANTS

Several authors have described the ethical standards of those who work in the ID field (see Foxon, Richey, Roberts, & Spannaus, 2003; Klein, Spector, Grabowski, & de la Teja, 2004; Richey, Fields, & Foxon, 2001). Furthermore, professional associations such as the American Educational Research Association (AERA) and the American Psychological Association (APA) have identified ethical standards for researchers. These standards help to protect individuals who are asked to participate in a study and those who agree to do so.

Getting Approval to Conduct Research

U.S. federal regulations require that you obtain approval if you plan to collect data from participants by interacting with them or by implementing an intervention. Approval must be granted by an Institutional Review Board (IRB) or Independent Ethics Committee registered with the U. S. Office for Human Research Protections [see http://www.hhs.gov/ohrp/assurances] before soliciting participation or collecting any data. The approval process requires you to show how participants' rights as a human subject will be protected. Scholars who conduct design and development research may be exempt from certain requirements when they collect data on normal educational practices in established educational settings; however, it is always wise to consult with an IRB in your local area to determine requirements for your study.

Approval to conduct research must also be granted by the organization in which the study will be conducted. This involves getting permission from someone who has the authority to grant it. For example, a researcher who plans to collect data in a school setting may be required to get permission from a principal, a director of research and evaluation at the district level, or even the local school board. A researcher who wishes to study expert designers working in training department would likely need the permission of the training manager or head of human resources.

Finally, approval must be given by the actual participants in the study (or their parents or legal guardians, if minors are involved). Getting approval from research participants relates to the notion of informed consent.

Obtaining Informed Consent

Research participants have the right to informed consent. They should be informed of any potential physical, psychological, or social risks related to participation in the study, and told if their responses could damage their employability, financial standing or reputation. Participants should also be told if the results of the study will be released to anyone in their organization or company, even if the results are anonymous and data are aggregated. After they have been informed of all potential risks and consequences, participants should have the right to decline.

Avoiding Coercion

Coercion is when an individual is unable to decline participation in a research study. It can occur when someone with authority in an organization requires employees or students to take part in a study. Researchers should be attuned to subtle coercion, such as social pressure that some participants may be unable to avoid. To avoid coercion, participants should be told they have the right to decline involvement in the study and be allowed to withdraw from it at any time without penalty. For example, in Adamski's (1998) research, he provided the following written statement for participants:

> If for any reason you do not wish to participate in the study, you may withdraw at any time. Your participation is completely voluntary. Your withdrawal will have no effect upon your class grade nor will any entry on your student record be made indicating your withdrawal. (p. 304)

Maintaining Confidentiality and Ensuring Anonymity

Design and development researchers sometimes uncover problems in organizations or observe individuals who are doing a less than adequate job. Researchers may also ask participants to reveal their innermost thoughts and feelings about the organization or the people in it. In such cases, you should ensure participants that results will remain anonymous (often through the use of pseudonyms) and that data will be aggregated instead of reported for each individual. It is also important to maintain confidentiality to extent allowed by law (you must report criminal behavior). Information that is obtained from participants should not be disclosed without their permission.

Here are two ways that design and development researchers have met this criteria of ethical research. Jones (1999) gave this statement to her participants:

> The information that you provide in the survey or during the audio taped interview will be anonymous. When completing the survey, feel free to omit any questions. Please do not discuss your comments with anyone other than [the researcher]. At the conclusion of this study the audiotapes will be destroyed. None of the information that you provide will be used for performance appraisal by the principals of [their organization]. (p. 125)

Cowell (2001) ensured her participants of confidentiality and anonymity with this statement that they signed:

> I understand that my confidentiality will be maintained by the assignment of a code number to my answers and that the information will only be used for data collection. No direct link will be made to any of the information in my data set, and in no way will the code number by reported in a manner that can identify me. After all data are collected, the interview material and raw data will be destroyed. Further, I understand that the only reference to my interview will be a listing in citation format and an acknowledgement of my contribution to the research project, unless I request total anonymity. (p. 126)

LOOKING AHEAD

This chapter has focused on issues related to the selection of participants and settings for a design and development study. As we discussed, participants vary widely in design and development research; there are many techniques that can be used to select a sample of people, projects, and organizations to study. Furthermore, issues related to the setting and its selection can have a profound effect on your research. We provide a checklist below to assist in the selection of settings and participants for your design and development study.

Once participants and settings have been selected, it is time to collect data. The next chapter provides detailed information on the common data collection tools and strategies used in design and development research.

A CHECKLIST FOR SELECTING PARTICIPANTS AND SETTINGS IN A DESIGN AND DEVELOPMENT STUDY

1. Identify the range of settings where your design and development study could be conducted.
2. Select the setting that includes the conditions and elements necessary to answer your research questions by addressing:
   - Does the design and development research problem exist in the setting?
   - Are all of the various aspects of the situation that you want to study readily identifiable in the setting?
   - Is it feasible and practical to conduct the study in the setting?
3. Identify and select human participants (e.g., designers, developers, subject matter experts, clients, learners) and non-human participants (e.g., organizations & projects) to include in the study based on your research questions.
4. Follow prescribed quantitative or qualitative sampling techniques to identify a sample of participants from a population of interest.
5. Implement ethical guidelines and standards to protect human participants by addressing the following questions:
   - Have you obtained approval to conduct the study from a registered Institutional Review Board (IRB) or Independent Ethics Committee?
   - Have you of obtained organizational permission to conduct the study?
   - Have you avoided coercion and obtained informed consent from participants?
   - Have you established procedures to maintain confidentiality and ensure the anonymity of participants?

7

Collecting Data in Design and Development Research

While it may seem that the bulk of planning your design and development study should be complete, another major task lies in front of you: planning for data collection. Clearly, your data collection plans were started as you were devising the research design of your study; however, as with so many things, the activity seems to expand as you near the actual task. Detailed data collection plans are intertwined with issues of measurement, instrumentation, and specific research strategies. As with research design and participant selection, there are aspects of collecting data in design and development research projects that pose problems different from those confronted by other types of research projects. This chapter will concentrate on these distinctive features as we examine:

- Critical design and development research data.
- Data collection instruments.
- Technology-based data collection strategies.
- Data collection issues.

CRITICAL DESIGN AND DEVELOPMENT RESEARCH DATA

The data researchers collect depend on the nature of their research questions and hypotheses. In design and development research, however, questions and hypotheses often have unique variations that make certain types of data more relevant than in other types of research. Here, we will examine such data as they relate to:

- Descriptions of key project components.
- Design, development and implementation contexts.
- In-progress projects.
- Product evaluations.

Profile Data

Design and development research projects typically have two types of participants. The first category consists of all of the people who may be involved in a particular project. As discussed in Chapter 6, design and development studies may have a broader range of these types of participants than is typical of other types of research. They often include not only designers and developers themselves, but also design teams, clients, instructors, and learners. However, design and development studies also have another type of participant: the project itself.

Projects can be profiled in terms of their scope, the resources available to the project, and the nature of the particular product to be produced. Of particular importance are records of the time, monies, facilities, equipment, and personnel that had been allocated to the project. Key product data include descriptions of its scope, content, delivery mechanisms, and intended use.

Researchers routinely collect demographic and profile data from project participants. Design and development research is no different; however, the type of data typically collected may vary from that which is collected in other research projects. For example, in addition to routine demographic data such as age, gender, and ethnicity, work experience has proven to be a critical piece of information in many design and development studies. This pertains to designers, instructors, clients, and adult learners alike.

Table 7–1 presents an array of specific profile data critical to design and development researchers. This table should give you a more complete picture of the types of profile data you might want to collect in your study.

One piece of profile data that is of particular importance in much current design and development research is the expertise of the designer. Increasingly,

TABLE 7–1.
Critical Profile Data in Design and Development Research

Type of Data	Topic	Sample Variables of Interest
Profile Data: Participants	Designer/developers	Demographics: Age, Gender, Ethnicity
		Education: Highest Degree & Majors
		Years of Design Experience
		Level of Expertise
		Current Job: Type of Employer, Primary responsibility, Where products are used
	Design Team	Team Size
		Team Make-Up
	Clients	Years of Work Experience
		Work Experience with ID Projects & Teams
		Education: Highest Degree & Majors
	Learners	Demographics: Age, Gender, Ethnicity, Work Experience, Educational Background Technology Experience
	Instructors	Demographics: Age, Gender, Ethnicity
		Education: Highest Degree & Majors
		Years of Instructional Experience
Profile Data: ID Project	Scope	Number of Allocated Personnel
		Number of Targeted Learners
		Cost
		Work Time Allocated
	Resources	Design Facilities
		Design Equipment Available
		Delivery Equipment Available
		Equipment Quality
	Product Characteristics	Type of Product & Delivery
		Instructional Content
		Average Time-on-Task
		Intended Use: Cultural Setting, Type of Organization

this is a focal point of many studies and consequently deserves special consideration here. Even with the increased attention given to this variable, the definition of expertise is not standard across projects. A simple explanation of expertise commonly given is that it is either predicted by innate factors, or is based upon longs periods of practice (Ericsson, 2004). The innate ability explanation, while intuitively logical, has not been supported by research; however, the sustained practice explanation has been verified (Ericsson & Charness, 1994). Furthermore, Simon and Chase's (1973) studies of expert chess players is also seen as a rationale for concluding that an expert has at least 10 years of full-time experience in a given field. This logic has been widely used in many studies of expert designers as a rationale for classifying participants as either novices (e.g., those with less than 10 years of experience) or experts (e.g., those with more than 10 years of experience).

Even though this guideline provides a clear technique for identifying experts and measuring expertise, there are nagging concerns. Does experience always result in expertise? Are there persons who demonstrate expert performance who are not generally recognized or who have only limited formal work experience? Does expert behavior really represent a performance plateau, or is there a continuous path of growth in some people throughout their lives?

Ericsson (2004) provides an alternative to the "10-year rule" approach to defining expertise. This first involves identifying tasks that are representative of "superior, reproducible behavior" (p. 78). Experts, then, are persons who exhibit these behaviors, not simply persons with a given amount of work experience.

This approach then requires that design and development scholars seek out these behaviors from the designer expertise literature. For example, Rowland (1992) and Perez and Emery (1995) reported that expert designers:

- Spend a large amount of time in problem analysis, viewing the problem as ill-defined, and challenging the "givens."
- Consider a wide-range of design solutions and arrive at the chosen solution through a problem-solving process.
- Use a combination of interventions to solve performance problems.

Rather than using the 10-year rule to identify expert designers, the far better approach is to place designers on an expertise continuum based upon an analysis of their design behaviors (actual or self-reported). While this approach is more complex, the data (and the subsequent conclusions) will be more credible.

Context Data

By now you've probably noticed that context is as critical a part of many design and development studies as it is critical to ID projects themselves. At least three different contexts have major implications for design and development research: (a) the environment in which the design and development takes place, (b) the environment in which the intervention is implemented, and (c) the performance environment in which skills and knowledge are applied. Each of these contexts widely vary.

Design environments are characterized as much by the nature of their parent organizations as by their own descriptive factors. The parent organization's industry and size can be key factors that shape the department responsible for ID. They often influence not only the size of the ID unit and the scope of its work, but also the predominant type of education and training programs produced. For example, education and training in the technology-oriented aircraft industry is likely to be computer-based, while the professional development of teachers is typically conducted in workshops.

Tessmer and Richey (1997) identified many contextual factors that research has shown to influence the instructional design process. Their discussion of the instructional and transfer contexts is especially relevant to design and development research projects. The physical aspects of the instructional setting have much to do with the type of program that is likely to be successfully delivered; however, organizational resources and constraints also shape the instructional context. These not only include obvious factors such as supplies and equipment, but also other, more subtle factors such as education and training incentives.

The factors that influence the extent to which training is likely to be applied on-the-job are heavily influenced by organizational climate. Supervisor, coworker, and employee attitudes have a major impact on whether instructional content is applied or forgotten. See Table 7–2 for context data that may be relevant to your design and development research study.

In-Progress Project Data

We believe that the collection of in-progress data is critical to understanding the nature of design and development. While many researchers collect retrospective data on project procedures and activities, it is far less common for them to systematically gather data as the design and development is progressing. These data are critical to accurately understanding the nature of design and development.

There are a variety of types of in-progress project data that can be collected, but essentially, most can be traced to designers and developers, clients, or in some cases, to subject matter experts (SMEs). Table 7–3 presents in-progress data that are most common in design and development research.

The data required by design and development studies are project-dependent; however, much is common across projects and across studies, especially those pertaining to work performance and attitudes. Work logs kept by designers, developers, and even clients and SMEs are invaluable, as are actual work samples from various stages of the project. The reactions and opinions of all of the key players play a critical role in determining the success of a project. It is important to describe these in an effort to aid future projects.

It is also important to gather data focused upon difficulties that have arisen for designers and developers during the course of the project. Under what constraints were they operating? What resources were used, and what additional

TABLE 7–2.
Critical Context Data in Design and Development Research

Type of Data	Topic	Sample Variables of Interest
Context Data: ID Project	Design & Development Environment	Parent Organization: No. of Employees, Type of Industry, No. of Training Departments, No. of Training Employees ID Staff Size No. of ID Projects per Year Number of Learners Served Predominant Type of Training Produced Predominant Training Methodology Resources Available Constraints Typical
Context Data: Product/Program Implementation	Instructional Context	Sensory Conditions: Acoustics, Temperature, Lighting Seating Arrangements Learning Schedules Organizational Support: Equipment & Facilities, Released Time, Teaching Assistants, Rewards
	Transfer Context	Supervisor Support Co-Worker Support Opportunities for Transfer Performance Cues Present Motivation to Transfer: Perceptions of Utility, Incentives Resources Available

ones were needed? Data such as these may not be difficult to collect; however, records of failures and confusion can be more sensitive and, consequently, harder to collect. These data, however, are often the most important to study.

Design cycle time is one type of in-progress data commonly collected in design and development research due to the concerns many have with the time required to employ systematic ID processes. Measuring cycle time can be particularly vexing, however, because of the difficulties in accurately identifying the beginning and end of a project's design and development cycle. Project beginnings can vary. They may be:

- When a project proposal is started.
- When a proposal is funded or when the billing starts.
- When an assignment is given to a department, team or individual.

TABLE 7–3.
Critical In-Progress Data in Design and Development Research

Type of Data	Topic	Sample Variables of Interest
In-Progress Project Data: Designer/ Developers	Designer/Developer Performance	Daily Log: Tasks Completed, Time-on-task, Decisions Made, Persons Met/Consulted, Resources Used
		Extent to which ID & Org. Standards were Met
		Model Use: Ease, Flexibility, Adaptability
		Project Cycle Time: Overall Project, Separate Phases
		Product Samples: Prototypes, Screen Captures
	Designer/Developer Problems	Confusion: Process, Directions, Language
		Constraints: Time, Technical Skills, Conflicting Information
		Failures: Miscommunications, Equipment Malfunctions, Final Product
		Additional Needs Examples, Explanations, Equipment, Other Resources
	Designer/Developer Attitudes	Opinions of ID Models & Processes
		Opinions of the Learning Process
In-Progress Project Data: Clients	Client Tasks	Daily Logs: Decisions Made, Tasks Completed, Persons Met
		Information Provided
	Client Attitudes	Opinions: ID Processes, Proposed Solution, Final Product, Working Relationships
In-Progress Project Data: Subject Matter Experts	SME Tasks	Daily Logs: Tasks Completed, Persons Met, Data Provided, Recommendations Made
		Constraints

Similarly, project endings can vary. They may be:

- When a product is completed and delivered to the client in keeping with the contract.
- When a product is completed with revisions based upon the formative evaluation.
- When the summative evaluation of the product is complete.

In addition, there are other definition issues involved. For example:

- Is your cycle time to be measured in days, weeks, or months?
- Is your cycle time to be defined as the elapsed time between the start and finish of a project, or is it the sum of the actual work time of all involved?

The researcher must resolve all of these issues before collecting cycle time data.

Try-Out Data

Finally, design and development researchers, like designers themselves, collect product evaluation data from learners and instructors. In many respects, designers and researchers are interested in the same types of evaluation data. All are interested in data that describe the performance of the major players, and data that explain the success or failure of the product. Table 7–4 presents those data that are most commonly collected to accomplish these tasks.

The one thing that may be of unique interest to researchers is instructor performance data, which can be found in their work logs or gathered through observations. What does it take for the instructional products or programs to be effectively used? How much preparation time is necessary? How much teaching time? What modifications must be made?

All of this information creates a rich base of data from which a researcher can draw conclusions about the design and development processes. They create a quantitative and qualitative foundation for design and development practice.

DATA COLLECTION INSTRUMENTS

Researchers who study design and development tend to use a wide variety of data collection instruments. For example, McKenney (2002) employed six categories of data collection tools in her product development study, but she employed a total of 108 different instruments. Figure 7–1 shows the array of data collection instruments from the McKenney study. In addition, this figure shows where each instrument was used in the design and development process.

This display highlights the critical role that data collection instruments play in a design and development research project. While we are not going to address the basic principles of instrument design here, some data collection

TABLE 7–4.
Critical Try-Out Data in Design and Development Research

Type of Data	Topic	Sample Variables of Interest
Try-Out Data: Learners	Prerequisites	Content Knowledge
		Learning & Basic Literacy Skills
		Technology Skills
	Background Experiences	Cultural Background
		Education & Training Experience
		Work Experience
		Experience with Target Delivery System
	Performance	Achievement Scores (Pretest & Posttest)
		Delayed Retention Scores
		On-the-Job Behavior
	Attitudes	Attitudes Toward Delivery System
		Reactions to Product/Program
Try-Out Data: Instructors	Prerequisites	Content Knowledge
		Teaching Skills
		Technology Skills
	Background Experiences	Cultural Background
		Education & Training Experience
		Work Experience
		Experience with Target Delivery System
	Teaching Evaluations	Explanations of Content
		Enthusiasm & Motivation
		Facilitating Discussions & Promoting Interaction
		Objectivity & Fairness
	Attitudes	Attitudes Toward Delivery System
		Attitudes Toward Learners
		Reactions to Product/Program
	Work Records	Preparation Time
		Product/Program Modifications Made
		Teaching Time per Objective

tools are so commonly used in design and development research that they do deserve special mention. Following, we will discuss and provide some examples of:

- Work logs.
- Surveys and questionnaires.
- Interview protocols.
- Observation guides.

Phase	Cycle	Interview & Walkthrough Schemes	Questionnaires	Discussion Guides	Observation & Demo Scheme	Logbooks	Document Analysis Checklists
Analysis	LR			DG-SEITT1.4	D-NL1.1 D-AMSTIP.2 D-TEAMS1.3		
	SV	IS-UB.6 IS-TEAMS2 7	Q-SAARMSEa.5 Q-SAARMSEb.5 Q-SAARMSEc.5	DG-SAARMSE.5 DG-UB.6			
Design Development and Formative Evaluation	P1	W-DEV1.8 IS-PSU/UGA/USA.9 W-NL2.10		DG-NL3a.11 DG-NL3b.11 DG-NL3c.11 DG-NL3d.11	D-PSU.9		
	P2	W-DEV2.12	Q-TEAMS3.14	DG-TEAMS3.14	D-SEITT2.13 O-TEAMS3:14		DA-TEAMS3:14
	P3	W-DEV3.15 IS-SEITT4.19 IS-TEAMS4.20 IS-UNESCO1.21 IS-PTLC.22	Q-SEITT4a.19 Q-SEITT4b.19 Q-SEITT4c.19 Q-TEAMS4a.20 Q-TEAMS4b.20 Q-TEAMS4c.20 Q-TEAMS4d.20 Q-TEAMS4e.20 Q-UNESCO1a.21 Q-UNESCO1b.21 Q-PTLCa.22 Q-PTLCb.22 Q-PTLCc.22 Q-PTLCd.22 Q-PTLCe.22 Q-RSA1a.23 Q-RSA1b.23 Q-RSA1c.23 Q-RSA2.24	DG-SW.16 DG-SEITT4.19 DG-UNESCO1.21 DG-PTLC.22 DG-RSA1.23 DG-RSA2.24	D-UN.17 D-SEITT3.18 O-SEITT4.19 O-TEAMS4.20 O-UNESCO1.21 O-PTLC.22 O-RSA1.23	L-SEITT4.19 L-UNESCO1.21 L-RSA1.23	DA-SEITT4.19 DA-TEAMS4.20 DA-UNESCO1.21
	P4	W-DEV4.25 IS-SHOMAa.30 IS-SHOMAb.30 IS-SHOMAc.30	Q-NAM.26 Q-CETa.27 Q-CETb.27 Q-SEITT5a.28 Q-SEITT5b.28 Q-UNESCO2.29 Q-SHOMAa.30 Q-SHOMAb.30 Q-SHOMAc.30 Q-SHOMAd.30	DG-NAM.26 DG-CET.27 DG-SEITT5.28 DG-UNESCO2.29	O-CET.27 O-SEITT5.28 O-UNESCO2.29 O-SHOMAa.30 O-SHOMAb.30	L-UNESCO2.29	DA-SHOMA.30
Evaluation	FE		Q-TEAMS5a.31 Q-TEAMS5b.31 Q-NL3.32 Q-NSDSI.33	DG-TEAMS5.31 DG-NL3.32 DG-NSDSI.33	O-TEAMS5.31 O-NL3.32 O-NSDSI.33	L-NSDSI.33	DA-TEAMS5.31 DA-NL3.32 DA-NSDSI.33
	Qu		Q-QUERY.34				

Legend

LR	=	Literature review	FE	=	Final evaluation	DG	= Discussion guide
SV	=	Site visits	Qu	=	Query	O	= Observation scheme
P1	=	Prototype 1	IS	=	Interview scheme	D	= Demonstration guide
P2	=	Prototype 2	W	=	Walkthrough scheme	L	= Log book
P3	=	Prototype 3	Q	=	Questionnaire	DA	= Document analysis checklist
P4	=	Prototype 4					

FIGURE 7–1. An overview of data collection tools used in McKenney (2002). Reprinted with permission of Susan McKenney.

Work Logs

Work logs are common design and development data collection instruments. They can be used for collecting data that relate to both current and past projects, although they are most commonly used for "in-progress" projects. Their most typical use is with designers and developers; however, there are some studies that also use work logs to collect client and instructor data. Work logs typically document the precise nature of tasks and decisions made during the various design and development phases, time expended, tools used, and reactions to the process.

We are presenting two examples of work logs here. The instrument directed toward designers and developers shown in Fig. 7–2 was used in Forsyth's (1998) model use and validation study. It is very general and open-ended. Instruments with this open structure are often used by participants to record data as they are working on a given ID project.

In contrast, the designer/developer work log presented in Fig. 7–3 is directed toward very specific design tasks. This instrument structure was used by Jones and Richey (2000) to collect retrospective data. The specific design tasks serve as cues to help respondents recall the particular approach they used when completing each task. If possible, retrospective work logs should be used only in relation to fairly recently completed projects. Even then, researchers should use verbal cues or key project documents to stimulate participant's memories of their work.

It is possible to gather very specific time and task data with the first instrument. On the other hand, retrospective time data are more likely be cast in terms of days, rather than hours. It should be noted that in both of the studies using these work logs, these data were supported by a follow-up, in-depth interview to clarify and expand these entries.

Date/Time	General Activity	Reactions	Tools/Resources Used	Lessons Learned

FIGURE 7–2. Basic designer/developer work log for in-progress projects. Reprinted with permission of Janice Forsyth.

Task*	Description of this task in your project	Duration
Identify audience		
Identify instructional need		
Identify content, tasks, process, etc.		
(The instrument task list continues here.)		
Review the prototype with customer & revise as needed		
Obtain agreement on prototype and freeze content		
Complete the remaining components, including user interface, screen design, page layout, etc.		
Pilot test the product		
Revise the product		
Deliver product to customer, including client reaction		

*This is only a partial listing of the tasks shown in the original instrument.

FIGURE 7–3.   Task-oriented designer/developer work log for past projects. Reprinted with permission of Toni Jones.

Surveys and Questionnaires

Surveys and questionnaires are used throughout many design and development studies.[1] In the McKenney (2002) research, for example, 35% of her data collection instruments were questionnaires—the largest category of tools she utilized. These tools are used for a very wide range of research functions. They can be used to collect data such as participant demographics, attitudes of designers and learners, and evaluation information.

Figures 7–4 and 7–5 show portions of two survey instruments used in design and development research. Figure 7–4 was used in Richey, Fields, & Foxon's (2001) study to collect designer profile data. Many of these questions could be modified and used for collecting instructor demographic data. As is typical of such instruments, the questions are quantitative in nature and close-ended to facilitate quick analysis.

_____

[1]There are a number of excellent books on survey research and designing survey instruments. For example, see Sage Publication's *Survey Research Methods* (3rd Ed.) by Floyd J. Fowler, Jr. (2002).

1. Education: ✓ *Check highest level completed.*
   (1) ☐ High School Diploma or Equivalent
   (2) ☐ Some College/University
   (3) ☐ Bachelor's Degree
   (4) ☐ Master's Degree
   (5) ☐ Educational Specialist Degree
   (6) ☐ Ed.D. / Ph.D.
   (7) ☐ Other

   ✓ *Check **one**.*
2. Do you have a degree in instructional design or a related field?   (1) ☐ No   (2) ☐ Yes
   If related, identify.

3. Gender: (1) ☐ Male   (2) ☐ Female

4. Age: (1) ☐ 20-30   (2) ☐ 31-40   (3) ☐ 41-50   (4) ☐ 51-60   (5) ☐ 61 +

   ✓ *Check **one**.*
5. Indicate the primary region in which you work. *If other, identify.*
   (1) ☐ United States and Canada
   (2) ☐ Latin America, including Mexico
   (3) ☐ Africa
   (4) ☐ Asia
   (5) ☐ Australia and New Zealand
   (6) ☐ Europe
   (7) ☐ Middle East
   (8) ☐ Other

   ✓ *Check no more than **two***
6. What is your primary design job focus? *If other, identify.*
   (1) ☐ Design
   (2) ☐ Development
   (3) ☐ Evaluation
   (4) ☐ Management
   (5) ☐ Research and/or ID Teaching
   (6) ☐ Other

7. How many years have you been in the field of instructional design?   Years:_____

   ✓ *Check **one**.*
8. What portion of your time on the job is devoted to performing and/or managing instructional design?
   (1) ☐ 20% or less
   (2) ☐ 21-40%
   (3) ☐ 41-60%
   (4) ☐ 61-80%
   (5) ☐ 81-100%

   ✓ *Check **one**.*
9. Where are the products of your work typically used?   (1) ☐ In my own organization   (2) ☐ In another organization

10. To what type of organizational setting does your work typically relate?
    (1) ☐ Business/Industry
    (2) ☐ Health Care
    (3) ☐ Education
    (4) ☐ Govt./Military
    (5) ☐ Multiple Settings
    (6) ☐ Other

FIGURE 7–4.   Sample designer characteristic survey.

Figure 7–5 speaks to product evaluation issues. This instrument was used by McKenney (2002), and has questions that are both open and closed. Many studies use questionnaires simpler than that found in Fig. 7–5 to collect learner reaction and attitude data. However, these items often still use a similar Likert-type scale.

There are many other uses of surveys and questionnaires. Some survey-like instruments can serve as the basis of a document analysis. Many design and development studies include an examination of extant (i.e., still existing) data.

Reflective questionnaire non-science teachers

In this questionnaire we will ask you some questions about your satisfaction about the lesson plan you constructed and the process you followed. In addition, we will ask you some questions about the practicality of CASCADE-SEA. Finally we will ask you some questions about the manual you have used. Although you will be invited to fill out your name, we stress that all information will be handled confidentially.

Attention: In case of a '1 2 3 4 question'; you are asked to encircle the number that comes closest to your opinion about the concerning aspect.

1. Name ....

2. What do you think of the lesson plan you have constructed?

a.	Complete	1	2	3	4	Incomplete
b.	Easy to carry out	1	2	3	4	Difficult to carry out
c.	Usable	1	2	3	4	Not Usable

3. How did the construction process proceed?

a.	Many problems	1	2	3	4	No problems
b.	It was not realisable within time	1	2	3	4	It was realisable within time
c.	I did not have sufficient experience to do the task	1	2	3	4	I had sufficient experience to do the task

4. Did you get support from others during the use of CASCADE-SEA?

❑ No*(please turn towards question 5)*
❑ Yes

e.	Who did provide help? ....
f.	What was the reason for asking help? ....
g.	What kind of help did you get? ....
h.	Were you satisfied with the help? ....
	Yes, because, ...
	No, because, ...

5. What do you think of the practicality of the support that CASCADE-SEA gives you?

a.	Clear	1	2	3	4	Not clear
b.	Enough	1	2	3	4	Not enough
c.	Easy to use	1	2	3	4	Difficult to use

FIGURE 7–5.   Sample product evaluation survey. Reprinted with permission of Susan McKenney.

The task becomes essentially one of using a structured instrument to "survey" the document to gather data pertaining to topics such as:

- Product characteristics.
- Evidence of design tasks completed.
- Evidence of design and development decisions made.
- On-the-job behavior related to the instruction or the intervention.

Interview Protocols

Currently, much design and development research uses qualitative research designs that rely to a great extent upon interview data. Designers, clients, instructors, and even learners or users are all interviewed at times. These data allow the researcher to get a clear understanding of events, to determine why they occurred, and to gather data from participants about their thoughts and beliefs.

In many respects, the interview protocol is simply an open-ended questionnaire. The protocol is especially critical with long interviews, as is typical in many design and development studies. It establishes controls on the interview process, ensuring that all content is covered and that similar prompts are used with all participants. A structured interview protocol, however, does not prevent the exploratory, extemporaneous nature of a good interview (McCracken, 1988).

Visscher-Voerman's (2000) study of design approaches in training and education was based upon a series of repeated designer interviews. These interview questions would be typical of those collecting retrospective project data. This protocol essentially involves a detailed walk through the design and development process as it occurred. The detailed questions serve not only as a response stimulus, but also as a method of ensuring reliable and comparable data. A portion of Visscher-Voerman's interview protocol is presented in Fig. 7–6.

Interviews can also take other routes. Cowell (2001), for example, embedded the critical incident technique into her interviews that were directed towards understanding needs assessment practices. Figure 7–7 displays a portion of this interview protocol. The interview continued by focusing upon the context of the needs assessment, and the designer competencies required to be successful in needs assessment. The Cowell interview process also included the use of surveys to (a) select appropriate participants, (b) gather designer demographic and general needs assessment strategy data, and (c) prepare the participant for the upcoming interview. These surveys, plus the use of reminder phone calls, paved the way for a successful interview experience.

Observation Guides

Design and development researchers at times collect data by direct observation. Typically, this involves observing one or more of the following:

- Designers and developers as they work.
- Instructors employing instructional products or tools in their teaching.

1. Design Process

  • Start of a project
      i. How did the project get started?
     ii. What was done first when the project was initiated?
    iii. What activities were conducted (analysis, problem definition, etc.)?
     iv. Did you make a program of demands? Or a planning [document]?
      v. What were they like?
     vi. What did you do next?
    vii. How did you know what to do?
   viii. How did the project evolve?

  • Problem Specification
      i. Was there a specific problem underlying the project?
     ii. What was the type of problem? (class of problems/problem types)
    iii. To what extent did the problem determine what needed to be done?

The instrument continues with additional interview questions.

FIGURE 7–6.   Sample designer interview questions.

• Learners using a newly produced instructional product.
• On-the-job performance of persons who have participated in a particular intervention.

Observation techniques can play multiple roles in a research design. Participant observation is a traditional form of ethnographic research. More generally, this can be viewed as a form of naturalistic research—the study of people doing what they normally do (Levine, 1992). In this sense, many design and development studies are naturalistic research; however, observation techniques are not necessarily qualitative in nature. Many observation systems are methods of "deriving quantitative descriptions or measurements of human behavior from direct observation of specified aspects of the behavior" (Medley, 1992, p. 1310).

Whether a quantitative or a qualitative approach is taken by the researcher, observations are controlled through the use of a preplanned data collection instrument. Quantitative approaches are often guided by standard forms that direct the researcher to look for specific behaviors. Often these guides are simple checklists, such as the one used by Ottevanger (2001). (See Fig. 7–8.)

Directions to interviewer: Please use the following guide to explore the informant's needs assessment activities in the form of a recent "critical Incident.

6. From your experiences, what is the recent project that you will use as an example?
   Probe: Why did you do the needs assessment?
   Probe: Was this project particularly demanding or was it ordinary and typical?

7. How did you first approach the needs assessment? What were **the major steps** in the needs assessment process?
   Probe: What were you thinking about during the process?
   Probe: What methods did you follow?
   Probe: What were you looking for? What were you assessing?

8. When did you perform the needs assessment?
   Probe: What would be the situation that you would reexamine the needs again at a later date?
   Probe: Do you follow the same methods or an alternative?

9. The customer may believe that this is an informal process, but you probably go in with formal questions. **What are some of the prepared questions** that you present to the customer?

10. What were some of your concerns while you conducted the needs assessment?
    Probe: What were your feelings and thoughts?

11. What **kind of information** was generated from the needs assessment?
    Probe: Is this information that you expected to generate according to your initial hunches or intuition?
    Probe: Why do you think this happened?

12. What would you have done differently?
    Probe: What lessons did you learn from your involvement in this project?

FIGURE 7–7.   A critical incident interview protocol with probes. Reprinted with permission of Diane Cowell.

Other, more elaborate observation systems exist. Medley (1992) identified four types of data typically recorded in observation systems: (a) instances and sequence of behaviors occurring within a given domain, (b) instances of behaviors that are viewed as indicators of the presence of a variable being studied, (c) aspects of the context that can explain the behaviors occurring, and (d) setting descriptions. Checklists, such as that used by Ottevanger (2001), emphasize the second type of data, but they could be modified to be more comprehensive. Moreover, these observation guides can be constructed to relate to many design and development projects, including those pertaining to both performance improvement aids and traditional instructional products.

Other observation instruments provide for researcher comments or more detailed verbal descriptions of the events being observed. These have a qualitative orientation. They may be as simple as McKenney's (2002) workshop

Curriculum Profile

Introduction to Lesson

A. Basic teaching skills and classroom management — yes / no / n/a
1. Teacher appears organised and ready to start
2. Teacher checks homework
3. Teacher asks/answers homework questions
4. Teacher discusses and reviews homework (where applicable)
5. Teacher introduces the lesson (and series, if applicable)
6. Teacher relates activities to previous/future lessons
7. Teacher illustrates lesson topic using a demonstration
8. Teacher introduces/explains key concepts
9. Teacher makes use of classroom aids (blackboard etc.)
10. Teacher makes reference to textbook (where applicable)
11. Teacher attempts to include inattentive learners
12. Teacher poses questions and waits for learners' answers
13. Teacher summarises introduction with preliminary conclusion

B. Learner-centred orientation — yes / no / n/a
1. Teacher asks guided questions to introduce lesson/activity
2. Teacher illustrates lesson topic by involving learners
3. Teacher asks learners for their own ideas (e.g. re: activity)
4. Teacher responds to learner ideas/questions
5. Teacher uses learners' ideas to illustrate lesson/activity
6. T. establishes the relevance of activity to learners' daily lives
7. Teacher encourages learners to ask questions
8. Teacher attempts to guide learners to conclusions/ideas

C. Subject Matter — yes / no / n/a
1. Teacher relays accurate information to learners
2. Teacher relays complete information to learners

Time allocated: _____ Actual time: _____

Body of Lesson

Lesson body start time: _____

A. Basic teaching skills and classroom management — yes / no / n/a
1. Teacher introduces the activity
2. Teacher has essential materials ready and organised
3. T. makes sure that materials are easily accessible to learners
4. Teacher explains how to use materials/equipment
5. Teacher moves around classroom
6. Teacher stimulates less motivated groups
7. Teacher responds positively to learner's questions/answers
8. T. maintains a positive learning environment during activity
9. Teacher effectively handles discipline problems
10. Teacher effectively handles timing difficulties
11. Teacher successfully improvises because time runs short
12. Teacher provides worksheets (where applicable)
13. Teacher's preparedness contributes to a "smooth" lesson

B. Learner-centred orientation — yes / no / n/a
1. Teacher groups learners for activity
2. T. assigns appropriate number of learners to each group
3. Teacher considers the member composition of each group
4. Teacher assigns various group roles to members
5. Teacher gives practical instructions to the groups
6. Teacher stresses safety instructions (where applicable)
7. Teacher tells students what the objectives are for the activity
8. Teacher allows students "room to choose" their own approach
9. Teacher observes how learners choose to approach activity
10. Teacher makes sure learners execute activity and use materials/equipment correctly
11. Teacher interacts with students during activities

FIGURE 7–8. Sample classroom observation checklist from Ottevanger (2000). Reprinted with permission of Wont Ottevanger.

116

Workshop observation checklist.
Date _____
Institution _____
Number of participants _____
Sitting arrangements _____

Guiding questions:

a) Is the instructional manual handy and easy to follow?

b) What is the attitude of the participants when working on the computers?

c) What major problems where being faced in the process of using CASCADE program-Learning to use the icons?
   ....
   ....
   ....
   ....
   ....

d) What effort did they do when some of the parts were not understood, e.g. did they ask help from each other or from the researcher?

e) What is the reaction of the participants after the CASCADE program?

f) What are the general views from the participants
   - Is the manual user friendly?
   - Is the program easy to use or need some training?
   - Was the time used to make the lesson materials enough or the program was lengthy?
   - Is it worthy of use in Tanzania?

FIGURE 7–9.   Sample open-ended observation instrument. Reprinted with permission of Susan McKenney.

observation form that seeks the answers to simple questions such as "What major problems were being faced in the process of using the CASCADE program?" These instruments are simple to use, but depend upon discerning observers with a clear understanding of the situations at hand. Figure 7–9 shows portions of this observation form.

As with other types of data collection, observation instruments are often used in combination with other types of tools. Participant surveys, for example, may precede the observation, and interviews are often conducted as a follow-up activity.

TECHNOLOGY-BASED DATA COLLECTION STRATEGIES

Currently, more and more data collection is being facilitated by technology. The computer is no longer simply a data analysis tool. It now creates possibilities for collecting accurate time data and product usability data. It provides opportunities to capture and store designer work data. It provides ways of gathering survey data in a speedy and cost effective manner. Here we will examine the role of:

- Web-based data collection.
- Software-based data collection.
- Laboratory-based data collection.

Web-Based Data Collection

Web-based surveys are rapidly becoming the norm in many areas of research. There is a wide variety of low-cost software that formats survey instruments for delivery over the Internet. Thus, it is possible to easily deal with participant samples from a wide geographical range, and from a broad range of work settings, if these populations can be easily connected to the Internet. In addition, these programs automatically create data files that are directly compatible with the major data analysis software programs. There are, nonetheless, some problems related to web-based data collection, including:

- Instrument design.
- Recruitment and sampling.
- Response rate.

Instrument design issues. Even though the average researcher can now take advantage of the various programs for constructing Web-based surveys, there are issues that are unique to these formats rather than paper formats. Orr (2005) has suggested tactics that address key survey instrument design concerns. These include:

- When surveys are constructed using a multi-page format, use "progress bars" to show how much further respondents have to go to complete the instrument.
- Use dictionary-recognizable words (i.e., no acronyms or all-capital abbreviations) in the subject headings to avoid being bounced back by junk mail filters.
- Simplify your pages by using a white background, consistent fonts, font sizes, and formats.
- Limit the use of animation, color, italics, and other visual features that can detract from the survey content.

Recruitment and sampling issues. It is possible for Web-based surveys to be distributed and followed-up in much the same way as one would handle paper surveys; however, it is increasingly common for researchers to post their surveys on Web sites, Listserves, or other message boards in an effort to recruit a widespread group of respondents. In some cases, this occurs because the larger population cannot be easily identified. While a larger sample will be more reliable than a smaller sample (Fowler, 2002), there are nonetheless difficulties with some large samples. Orr (2005) noted that "because undefined volunteer samples are non-representative, and are not randomly selected, the results cannot be generalized beyond these respondents" (p. 263).

The ideal approach is to have a predefined set of computer-savvy participants (and their e-mail addresses). In this situation, the sampling issues related to Web-based surveys are minimized; however, not all researchers have the luxury of easily identifying potential respondents. One approach then is to screen potential respondents to make sure that they belong to the target population before allowing them access to the survey. Another approach is to collect sufficient demographic data on respondents to determine who is appropriate and who should be removed from the database.

Response rate issues.　　There are concerns over the rate of response to surveys in all formats since this is an important source of survey error; however, special issues pertain to Web-based surveys, especially given the current proliferation of spam e-mail messages. If survey participants can be identified in advance, certain methods can be followed in an effort to prevent low response rates. The primary technique involves pre-survey contacts with the potential respondents. In Cook et al.'s study of Web and e-mail surveys (as cited in Orr, 2005), they found that response rates were most influenced by the number and personalization of contacts made both before the survey was delivered and after. This finding has been widely substantiated. Mass mailings to a distribution list without a pre-contact are more likely to have low response rates.

Moreover, Rossett (1999) identified another factor that can impact response rate, even with pre-contacts. This is when respondents question the anonymity and traceable trail of Web-surveys, especially those that may be connected to e-mail addresses. Researcher integrity and assurances of confidentiality are imperative. Even though, some surveys (which are ostensibly anonymous) are designed to have the results sent to the researcher's e-mail address with visible IP addresses. Ultimately, response rate can be a matter of trust.

However, what if the researcher does not have a pre-identified list of respondents? What if the survey is posted openly seeking respondents? Then what do you do to increase response rate? In these situations, traditional survey design principles are going to be most helpful. For example:

- Avoid surveys that are too long.
- Make efforts to distribute the survey to persons who are most interested in your topic.

- Avoid overly sensitive topics, if possible.
- Make the instrument easy to complete.
- Assure the respondents that the results are both anonymous and confidential.
- Offer incentives to complete the survey.

Software-Based Data Collection

Many design and development research projects rely on the ability of software programs to collect user data, as well as to perform their main functions. These capabilities are proving invaluable for studying all types of user behavior, whether the users are designers, developers, or learners.

What kind of data can be collected with these advanced pieces of software that have not been previously accessible to researchers? These new programs are capable of making digital records of user experiences. They record, for example, user interactions with Web sites and other products and materials. Learning paths and work time can be digitally recorded, and some software works in combination with camera and microphone arrangements to capture video and audio records of the users as they work. Screen captures can be collected to provide records of one's step-by-step progress in a design and development task. Thus, it is possible to collect precise "in progress" project data without relying solely upon work logs or interviews. Moreover, these data will provide records of the detailed decisions made throughout the progression of a given project.

These capabilities for digital observations can also be applied to end users of the newly developed products and programs. Thus, learner assessments and formative evaluations of product or programs can be made with far more accuracy and depth of data collection than has previously been possible. Table 7–5 shows a sample array of data that can be collected using these advanced technologies.

Laboratory-Based Data Collection

Some researchers using advanced technologies to collect data are working in a laboratory environment. For the most part, design and development research laboratories are found in universities and large research centers. These laboratories can vary widely in terms of levels of sophistication, and correspondingly, they can vary widely in terms of the financial resources required to build and maintain the facility.

The larger laboratories typically separate the researcher/observers from the participants relying upon software-based data collection tools that are supple-

TABLE 7–5.
Design and Development Process Data Accessible via Technology

Type of User	Data	Technology Used
Designer/Developer	Work Time	Data Acquisition Software
		Development Software
	Tasks Completed	Project Management Software
	Work Flow	Data Acquisition Software
	Screen Captures	Data Acquisition Software
	"Think Aloud" Records of Design Decisions	Voice Recognition Software
	Key Strokes and Mouse Clicks	Data Acquisition Software
	Facial Expressions, Comments & Movement During Work	Station-mounted Cameras
	Records of All Work Products	Back-up Files
	Verbal Records of Questions/ Problems/Insights	Voice Recognition Software
Learner/Performer	Learning Paths	Data Acquisition Software
		Multimedia Player Program
	Screen Captures	Data Acquisition Software
	Facial Expressions, Comments & Movement during Learning	Station-mounted Cameras
	Key Strokes and Mouse Clicks	Data Acquisition Software
	Verbal Records of Questions/ Problems/Insights	Voice Recognition Software

mented by a video system. They may even be connected to other research and development centers, so that researchers at remote locations can work in the laboratory as well. These arrangements facilitate collaborative research. Not surprisingly, such laboratories are usually supported and maintained by a large staff with many skills.

While much exciting research emanates from these large design and development laboratories, here we are describing a general structure for a small, less expensive laboratory that may be more adaptable to organizations with more modest funds. The laboratory presented here would currently cost under $50,000 to build. It would not have the most advanced hardware and software available, nor would it be able address all design and development issues. It would be a small laboratory that would permit data to be collected from up to four persons at a time; however, it is one that would serve as a good entry into this type of data collection.

Table 7–6 shows the manner in which such a laboratory could be outfitted. This table presents specifications for the researcher's station and the user station, as well as basic design and development equipment.

TABLE 7–6.
Sample Hardware and Software Specifications for a Basic Design and Development Research Laboratory

Type of Station	Hardware	Software
1 Researcher's Station	1 researcher's computer station	Base package of a data acquisition system
	1 microphone	Voice recognition program
		Professional edition of a survey development program
		Qualitative & quantitative data analysis programs
		Standard suite of productivity tools (inc. project management & flowcharting programs)
		PDF reader & writer
3 Standard User's Stations	3 participant/user computer stations	3 Standard suites of productivity tools
	3 microphones	3 Remote capture data acquisition programs
	3 station-mounted cameras	3 Standard suites of multimedia development & player programs
		1 voice recognition program
1 Station for User/Developer	1 participant/user computer station with double monitor	1 Remote capture data acquisition program
	1 microphone	1 Suite of productivity tools
	1 station-mounted camera	Standard suite of multimedia development & player programs
		Script editor program
		Video editing software
		Screen recording program
General Design & Development Productivity Tools	1 server with an external hard drive	
	1 color laser printer	
	1 scanner	
	1 32″ LCD display screen	
	1 digital camera	
	1 camcorder	

This laboratory could be housed in a room as small as 16 to 18 feet square. It would need five work stations large enough to accommodate the use of books and other work materials. Lighting, power capabilities, and acoustics would need to be appropriate for the research situation.

DATA COLLECTION ISSUES

You may think of data collection as a series of systematic techniques, as a matter of following clear-cut procedures. As with so many activities, however, there are more "shades of gray" than one would care to admit. This is especially true with design and development studies that deal with real-life projects. In this section we will explore some issues related to building a data set that is both accurate and complete.

Ensuring Data Integrity

Data triangulation. In qualitative and some mixed methods research, there is often an effort to take multiple measures of each phenomenon, event, or experience. If the findings from these measures are consistent, you can be more confident of the validity of your results (Brewer & Hunter, 2006). This is known as data triangulation. This technique is commonly used in design and development research.

Data triangulation is especially critical in design and development studies based upon participants' recollections of already completed projects. In these cases, memories should be supported by other participants or by a review of extant data. Therefore, in any retrospective study, researchers should intentionally collect data from multiple sources pertaining to each key aspect of the study. Without this, the data set could be biased and the subsequent findings open to question.

Self-reports. In addition to the effects of memory flaws, a data set can be biased because of a reliance upon self-reports. Self-reported data can take (roughly) two forms—reports of one's own perceptions and attitudes, and reports of past events. Such data are not uncommon in design and development research. Data describing on-the-job performances are often self-reported because both management and unions object to outside observers recording work performance. Past achievement records are self-reported because educational files are considered private and cannot be released to researchers. Work experience data are often self-reported because personnel files are sealed. There are many solid reasons for a researcher to use self-reported data, but questions are often raised as to their accuracy. Perceptions can be biased, and event reports can be challenged as second-hand information or, "hearsay." In many cases, participants may simply be providing the data that they think researcher wants to hear.

What should a researcher do to substantiate such data? In some situations, nothing can be done, other than being open about the limitations of the data set. Sometimes you can use data triangulation techniques to corroborate the data. One approach to data triangulation here is to conduct follow-up interviews with a sample of the participants to determine if there appear to be any deviations from the self-reported data. These interviews may also seek actual products to back up previously reported events.

In quantitative studies, you can use self-reported data for analysis after first determining if there is variance among the measures. For example, respondents may be asked to report on their college grade point averages (GPAs), and those GPAs are then correlated with on-the-job success measures. If there is variance in the set of GPA reports (even though they might be inflated), the ultimate correlations could still be valid, even though the foundational descriptive data were suspect. In all studies, however, the question of self-reported data must be resolved in some way.

Accommodating organizational restrictions. Sometimes the best data collection plans are thwarted by decisions of the participating organization. For example, transfer data are scheduled to be collected three months following the training session, but the company then has pressing deadlines to be met, and you can only collect the data either at six weeks or six months after training. Or you are going to conduct focus groups consisting of one representative from each department, and just before the session, two departments prevent their representatives from attending because of work pressures. Or halfway through a major organizational performance improvement study of a government agency, the agency becomes involved in a highly publicized negligence situation, leadership changes, and most participants become reluctant to give interviews to an outsider. There are many, many stories of research fiascos.

Researchers are often left with little recourse in these situations other than creative problem solving; however, minor changes in methodology can often be made to accommodate the rules imposed by the organization. It is necessary that all data be collected consistently and that they are comparable. For example, it may be possible in some situations to view the study as a type of time series design and compare the data before and after the intervention. What you must do is maintain the integrity of the data set.

Establishing Appropriate Data Sets

Data sets should be not only valid, but also appropriate. What does this mean? Assuming that the data set matches the demands of the research questions, the next question of appropriateness can be viewed as determining how much data you actually need. In most research, this is a matter of sampling. Many design and development researchers, especially those involved in product development studies, do not sample, but collect data during the entire course of the project. This can lead to huge quantities of data, and the question is "how much is really necessary?" The answers to this question are project-specific, but the more general principal is that researchers should carefully determine which data are essential to the research and which data only add marginally to a data set.

The next part of this dilemma is making sure that the data truly reflect all aspects of the target question. This can become more problematic for in-progress than for retrospective studies. One situation that can arise during a design and development study is when the project is not going well. What do you do if the project you are studying turns out to be a failure? Researchers building a truly appropriate data set would continue the data collection with the conviction that at times, the study of failure can reveal lessons as important as those learned from success stories. While this approach sounds reasonable, it is nonetheless difficult for many researchers to devote time to an unsuccessful project.

LOOKING AHEAD

For many, collecting data is the most interesting part of a design and development research study. It allows you to roll up your sleeves and interact with participants in their work setting. In this chapter, we have examined important types of data that are collected in a design and development study and have discussed the instruments that are often used to collect these critical data. We also suggested how technology can be used for data collection in design and development research. Following this chapter, we provide a checklist to help you plan for the collection of relevant and accurate data and to ensure the integrity of your data.

Once you have data in hand (or more likely, in several boxes), you must answer the questions "What does it mean? Why did all of those things happen? Are the findings what I expected?" After collecting data, you move into data analysis and interpretation. During this phase of the design and development study, you will be applying all of the skills that you have learned about handling both quantitative and qualitative data; you will be getting the "feel" of your data.

Perhaps one of the hardest parts of researchers' jobs is to make sense of their findings in such a way that enables others to learn from their experiences. In the next chapter, we will explore how your findings can contribute to the literature and to the knowledge base of the field. In addition, we will examine the range of conclusions that can emerge from design and development research on products, tools, and models.

A CHECKLIST FOR COLLECTING DATA
IN A DESIGN AND DEVELOPMENT STUDY

1. Identify data that are relevant to your design and development study by asking the following questions:
   - Should profile data be collected on participants and projects?
   - Should context data be collected on the design, instructional, and transfer environments?
   - Should in-progress or retrospective data be collected from designers, clients and SMEs?
   - Should evaluation data be collected to determine the impact, successes or failures of the project?
2. Use a wide variety of quantitative and qualitative data collection instruments in your design and development study.
3. Follow prescribed techniques for developing, testing, and validating your data collection instruments.
4. Use technology-based data collection strategies such as web-based surveys, computer software and design and development research laboratories.
5. Ensure the integrity of your data by asking the following questions:
   - Have you triangulated data especially when retrospective data are being relied on?
   - Have you substantiated self-report data?
   - Have you accommodated organizational restrictions imposed during data collection?
6. Establish the appropriateness of data sets by asking the following questions:
   - Have you collected only those data necessary to answer your research questions?
   - Does your data reflect all aspects of your research questions?

8

Interpreting Design and Development Findings

Research is about creating knowledge, and as such the goals of any research project are not simply to collect data but to derive meaning from the data. The process of extracting meaning from data is fraught with dangers of logic fallacies, personal biases, and professional blinders. It is also a process that can be filled with excitement and promise. This chapter pertains to interpreting your results, but even more importantly it pertains to understanding the full implications of your findings for both practice and theory. Specifically, we will focus upon:

- The contributions of design and development research.
- Interpreting product and tool research findings.
- Interpreting model research findings.
- Issues related to interpretation.

THE CONTRIBUTIONS OF DESIGN AND DEVELOPMENT RESEARCH

Fundamentally, we conduct research in an effort to expand the field's knowledge base, which will, in turn, impact practice. This is not a simple process, but one which ideally involves being aware of the field's current literature, having insights into the demands of the workplace, and having the foresight to envision new research that will facilitate disciplinary and professional progress. While few of us may be able to attain all of these goals, we can be mindful of them when interpreting the findings of design and development studies—both product and tool research and model research. The findings of both of these types of research can be understood in terms of how they:

- Expand the knowledge base.
- Lead to new research.
- Establish the foundations of new theory.

Expanding the Design and Development Knowledge Base

Interpreting your findings begins with understanding their role in the field. This contextualization process began early in your study when you described the problem your research was addressing. As we discussed in Chapter 2, these problems typically come from the workplace, or they relate to emerging technologies, or they may be associated with theoretical issues. However, these problems (and consequently your related findings) are also connected to the knowledge base of the field. For example, Ryan, Hodson-Carlton, and Ali (2005) conducted a study of online teaching which responded to pressures to design and implement online nursing courses at the university level. The findings of their research were discussed in terms of their implications for not only instructional practice, but also as an addition to the literature on model development. The findings can be understood in terms of their contribution to workplace problems as well as their contributions to the design and development knowledge base.

While design and development as a whole has a broad knowledge base (see Fig. 1–1 in Chapter 1), design and development research has the most influence on the section of the knowledge base labeled "Designer and Design Processes." Figure 8–1 shows how design and development findings greatly expand this part of the knowledge base.

The wide range of findings that emanate from both product and tool research and model research provide a rich source of information that can inform design and development theory and practice. It is clear from Fig. 8–1, however, that contextual data and findings that pertain to the setting in which the research takes place are instrumental to a general interpretation of the study. Product and tool development processes, for example, are greatly influenced by the climate, resources, and characteristics of the organization in

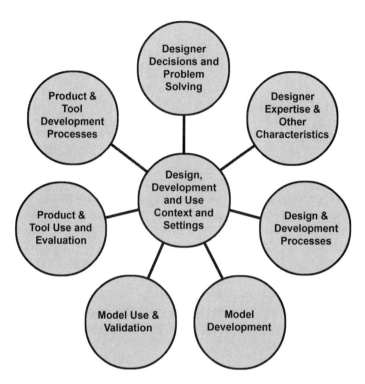

Figure 8–1.   Expanding the designer and design processes knowledge base through design and development research findings.

which these processes occur. The ways in which design and development models are used are similarly impacted by the nature of the settings.

However, context is not the only element to overlap with others; many of these findings are interrelated. One could argue that the knowledge base will only be fully understood when there is a large body of research that informs us of both the basic elements of design processes and the many relationships among these elements.

Creating Foundations for Design and Development Theory

To many, the ultimate objective of research is theory construction. Good research leads to more than a proliferation of facts. It should lead to the development of empirically based theory that can be used by practitioners and theorists alike. Design and development research is no different. A full understanding of design and development findings should include an appreciation of their role in the development of new theory or an awareness of how it supports or refutes existing theory.

Theory has been defined as sets of logically linked propositions or hypotheses that explain or predict events (Hoover & Donovan, 1995). Theory allows us to organize and summarize knowledge (Littlejohn, 1978), interpret data, and determine the larger meanings of research findings (Hoover & Donovan, 1995). It also provides direction for practice by suggesting workplace improvements. In essence, theory can describe, explain, predict, improve, or prescribe events.

For the most part, current theory specific to instructional design provides direction to all or parts of the design and development process. It can also predict the effects of various design and development strategies, or the impact environmental conditions and participants have on the design and development process.

However, theory construction rooted in design and development research findings can be difficult. Much of this research—essentially all of the product and tool research—is rooted in specific design and development projects. As such, the findings are to a great extent context-specific. The dilemma is this: How do you build generalized theory from context-bound data? George and Bennett (2005) provide some direction. In doing so, they site the advantages of the case-study method as a vehicle for identifying the following:

- The best indicators of a theoretical concept.
- New hypotheses.
- New variables.
- Rich explanations of causal relationships.

Other forms of qualitative research can have these same advantages. Even when specific individuals, groups, or events are studied, one can learn things that would apply to similar individuals, groups, or events (Berg, 2004). Consequently, design and development theory can be informed by contextualized findings as well as those generated by data derived from traditional sampling techniques.

Researchers use a multi-step process when seeking theoretical meaning from their findings. First, they must determine exactly what their findings are, and then discover and understand the relationships between these findings and those of other researchers. Finally, they must identify the general principles supported by this integrated knowledge base. In terms of design and development, this process can lead to narrow theories relating to particular phases or elements of the process. It can also lead to comprehensive theories that describe and explain the entire design and development process, as well as predict the impact of various strategies, participants, and conditions embedded in the process. It is critical, however, that these theories are supported by a *series* of studies, not simply isolated efforts. Ideally, the findings that support a particular theory would be replicated across settings and across populations.

Creating Foundations for Future Research

Research, especially research in relatively uncharted waters, plays an important role in creating interest in and providing direction for other explorations of similar topics and problems. This direction to some extent stems from reflecting upon, and gaining an understanding of, the findings of current research. It stems from thinking about what else the field needs to know and from thinking about what practitioners need to know. If a study (such as Rowland, 1992, or Perez & Emery, 1995) identifies distinctions between how experts and novices design instruction, what else do practitioners need to know to make this knowledge useful? Do they need to know how to teach novices to behave like experts? Do they need to know if more specific directions enable novices to behave like experts? These are new design and development research problems and questions. This reflection process is one phase of understanding the full implications of your findings.

Often these new research problems and questions are not obvious. A large portion of design and development research has a qualitative orientation, much of which is exploratory in nature. These types of studies often do not produce concrete answers to existing problems that can be widely generalized to other designers and to other settings. However, this research can lead to the identification of new problems and new questions. For example, Wang, Moore, Wedman, and Shyu (2003) conducted a qualitative formative evaluation of a knowledge-repository tool. The study led to information on revisions needed in the tool as expected. However, it also produced unexpected findings that could generate new research questions. The researchers learned of new ways the tool could be used by teachers and ways that the knowledge repository could be used to support teacher education programs in technology integration. They also learned how teachers can use narratives as a way of learning about technology integration and problem solving. None of these things had been anticipated in their research designs, but they were all ideas that can generate additional research. Wang et al. (2003) had developed deeper understandings of their findings than originally planned. At times, these expanded interpretations of research findings produce more than new questions. They produce new explanations of events, explanations that require subsequent empirical verification.

We have explored the general contributions that research can make to the field. There are, however, specific types of conclusions that typically emerge from design and development research in particular. Not surprisingly, these conclusions vary between product and tool studies and model studies. The next two sections will address how these conclusions can be derived. First, product and tool research will be considered, and then model research.

INTERPRETING PRODUCT AND TOOL RESEARCH FINDINGS

The conclusions emanating from research can take many forms. For example, they can be syntheses of descriptive data. They can be principles confirmed by statistical analyses and generalized to a larger population. They can be cause-and-effect determinations. They can be themes or patterns that emerge across cases. Or they can be lessons that have been learned from specific projects, as is characteristic of product and tool studies. These are the unique contributions of this type of design and development research.

Here we will explore the nature of a wide variety of conclusions that come from product and tool studies. Researchers typically have two major areas of interest when they study the design and development of products and tools. They are usually interested in either:

- Product and tool design and development processes.
- Product and tool use.

Inherent in each of these goals is an underlying concern with the ultimate quality of the product or tool. We will now examine an array of product and tool conclusions and the data which support them.

Lessons Learned about Product and Tool Design and Development Processes

When researchers address products and tool design processes, they are fundamentally concerned with which processes are best to employ and what conditions facilitate their use in an efficient and effective manner. These concerns, while simple on the surface, involve a wide range of complex factors pertaining to things such as:

- The intricacies of the final product.
- The complexity, scope, and resources of the design and development project.
- The manner in which the product is intended to be used.
- The capabilities and backgrounds of both the designer/developers and the product users.

TABLE 8–1.
Product and Tool Design and Development Process Conclusions
and Supporting Data

Major Types of Conclusions Drawn	*Key Types of Supporting Data*
• Recommended product and tool design and development processes • Conditions conducive to efficient product and tool design and development	• Product/Tool Characteristics • Project Profile (e.g., scope, resources available) • Participant Profiles (e.g., design/developer, design teams, clients, user/learners) • In-Progress Data (e.g., designer/developer performance, designer/developer problems, client tasks, SME tasks) • Work Samples & Project Documentation • Design and Development Environment (e.g., parent organization, design organization characteristics)

As we have seen, product and tool studies frequently employ methodologies such as case studies, observations, in-depth interviews, and evaluation. Sometimes, surveys and experimental designs are incorporated into the research. There are often multiple participants—not only designers and developers, but clients, SMEs, and others who might be involved in the design and development processes. Consequently, the resulting datasets are typically very large and include both narrative and numerical data. Table 8–1 shows the two major types of conclusions emanating from representative studies of product and tool design and development processes, and the key data upon which these conclusions are based.

The syntheses of such datasets can produce a wide range of conclusions as well as different types of conclusions. Usually they are simply the "lessons learned" from a particular product development project. These lessons provide answers to the study's original research questions. They are often based upon analyses of qualitative data resulting from less-structured research that is exploratory in nature. At times, these databases may also include quantitative descriptive data focusing on factors such as the backgrounds of the designers and the nature of the organization in which the product design project is occurring. Your understanding of these lessons learned is shaped by integrating *all* of the available data.

Lessons Learned about Product and Tool Use

Product and tool-use studies most frequently concern the use of instructional products or programs in schools or employee training situations. However, there are many studies that pertain to non-instructional products or tools. A study by Nguyen, Klein, and Sullivan (2005) is one example. This was an experimental study comparing the use of three types of electronic performance-support systems in a business and industry setting.

In these studies researchers ultimately want to be able to recommend the way in which products and tools should be used and the conditions that facilitate their use. However, they may also want to describe the impact of the product's use and then identify the conditions that will ensure such an impact. Finally, product-use research can produce data that leads to improvements in the product or tool itself—improvements that will enhance its effectiveness and its impact.

These are interpretations which depend upon multifaceted datasets and often complex research designs. The research may involve many of those same methods used to study product and tool design and development processes, such as case studies and in-depth interviews. However, they also rely upon evaluation research methods, surveys, structured expert reviews, and experimental designs.

These studies typically generate far more than the exploratory datasets that are common with case studies. Descriptive and explanatory data are also required. For example, full descriptions are needed of:

- The product or tool itself.
- The persons using the product (both learners, instructors, and other users when appropriate).
- The contexts (both instructional and transfer) in which the product are used.

In addition, product- or tool-evaluation data are needed so that explanations of product use can be ascertained. These data can provide the basis for statistical analyses which can identify relationships that exist between many of the aspects of product or tool use. For example, relationships can be identified between product use and many factors such as:

- Learner skill development and retention.
- Learner on-the-job use of the skills.
- Organizational improvement.
- Instructor characteristics.

Table 8–2 presents a summary of the various types of conclusions emanating from actual studies of product and tool use and the key data upon which these conclusions are based.

TABLE 8–2.
Product and Tool Use Conclusions and Supporting Data

Major Types of Conclusions Drawn	Key Types of Supporting Data
• Recommended procedures for product and tool use • Conditions that promote successful use of product or tool • Impact of product and tool use • Conditions that promote positive impact of product or tool • Suggested improvements in product or tool	• Product/Tool Characteristics • Participant Profiles (e.g., clients, user/learners, instructors) • Context Descriptions (e.g., instructional context, transfer context) • Evaluation Data (e.g., learner/user, instructor, organizational impact)

INTERPRETING MODEL RESEARCH FINDINGS

Model research generates conclusions that (unlike product and tool research) are more generalized and less context-specific. They are directed toward general principles which are applicable to a wide range of design and development projects. They all pertain to design and development models, rather than to products, programs, or tools. We have presented model research as a tripartite function encompassing model development, model validation, and model use. Correspondingly, the conclusions parallel this structure.

The conclusions of model research tend to be heuristics and broadly applicable principles. The "lessons learned" terminology is seldom used in relation to model research due to its more generalized nature. We will now explore the conclusions of each of the three facets of model research.

Understanding Model Development Findings

The findings of model development studies are obvious: new or enhanced design and development models. The manner in which these new models are constructed, however, is not always obvious. They can be created as a synthesis of data that captures the essence of:

- Actual design and development work, either current or retrospective.
- Related literature.
- A compilation of opinions of design and development experts.

The models resulting from these data tend to follow the structure of most ISD models. They are procedural models displayed in a graphical, often flow-chart-like, format. Often they are accompanied by supporting detail that provides further direction to the designer, such as a glossary of terms or lists of instructional-strategy options.

The new models or the model enhancements reflect what actually happens in natural design and development projects, what experts think should happen, or a combination of these two approaches. They are often adapted to the interests or constraints of a particular work environment.

Model development research can take many forms. Most approaches, however, establish baseline profile information describing the design and development environments, the types of projects undertaken, and the designer backgrounds. Then data are gathered that describe the actual tasks and sequence of tasks undertaken in a project. Designer decisions and problem-solving activities are identified. The procedural models are then derived by synthesizing and generalizing the tasks and conditions observed in projects occurring in natural work environments.

Other models are derived from a synthesis of the literature and expert input. Often these models are then tested in actual design and development projects and subsequently refined. The data, regardless of the research tactic, tends to be either exploratory or descriptive.

The conclusions (i.e., the models proposed) of a number of representative studies and the range of data used to devise these models are shown in Table 8–3.

TABLE 8–3.
Model Development Conclusions and Supporting Data

Major Types of Conclusions Drawn	Key Types of Supporting Data
• A new design and development model (comprehensive or specific phases) • An enhanced version of an existing design and development model	• Project Profile (e.g., scope, resources available) • Participant Profiles (e.g., designer/ developers, clients, SMEs) • Design and Development Environment (e.g. parent organization, design organization characteristics) • In-Progress or Retrospective Data (e.g., designer/developer performance, problems & attitudes, client tasks & attitudes, SME tasks) • Survey and Interview (e.g., design/ development experts, disciplinary literature)

Model development research can pertain to one project, such as Plass and Salisbury's (2002) model for Web-based, knowledge management systems; however, most new or enhanced models are rooted in data from multiple projects (e.g., Jones & Richey, 2000; Spector, Muraida, & Marlino, 1992) and many relate to a broad range of projects from many settings (e.g., Cowell, 2001).

Model development research can employ survey or interview techniques to gather designer-performance data from many settings. Single-setting data tends to be collected by interview, observation, or logs of in-progress data. Understanding the findings almost always involves synthesizing multiple sources of data. It may involve juxtaposing findings based upon quantitative analyses with those of qualitative analyses. Task-context interactions are usually important considerations.

Understanding Model Validation Findings

Most validation research addresses design and development models that are procedural. The conclusions of the studies then address questions such as:

- Is this the right way to design or develop a product under these circumstances? Are all of the steps included and in the right order?
- Is the model useable, practical, and cost-effective?
- Are the products resulting from this model's use effective and interesting?
- Does the product prompt routine behavior changes among its users? Are these changes beneficial to the larger organization?

These questions can be answered as a way of conducting an internal model validation (i.e., confirmation of the model's components and their sequence) or an external model validation (i.e., confirmation of the impact of the model). These two processes dictate the major types of validation conclusions that can be made.

Different datasets are typically used as a basis of these alternative types of model validation. Internal validation studies tend to produce descriptive data. These studies may rely on the same designer decision-making and problem-solving descriptions as were used in model development research. The validation conclusions may also depend upon expert opinion data drawn either from the literature, personal interviews, or structured techniques such as the Delphi Method. At times, model components are verified through studies of component effects. These studies often use self-reported survey data collected from users (either designers or learners). For the most part, internal validation data are descriptive in nature. Some data, especially those collected in the model component studies, may be exploratory.

External model validation decisions are overwhelmingly based upon evaluation data. They may lead to conclusions relating to the model's impact from

TABLE 8–4.
Model Validation Conclusions and Supporting Data

Major Types of Conclusions Drawn	Key Types of Supporting Data
• Confirmation of model components and sequence (i.e. internal validation)	• Survey and Interview (e.g. design/ development experts, disciplinary literature) • Designer/developer performance, problems, & attitudes • User perceptions and reports
• Confirmation of model impact (i.e. external validation)	• Evaluation Data (e.g. learner/user, instructor, organizational impact) • Context Descriptions (e.g. design, instructional, transfer)

the learner's point of view, or the instructor's, or the conclusions may concern the impact on the organization as a whole. The conclusions may also address the impact of the model on the designers or developers themselves. These conclusions often lead to interpretations of the model's usability, its practicality, or its effects on designer efficiency. External validation conclusions are based primarily on explanatory data. However, descriptive data are also important. For example, reports of designer, instructional, and transfer contexts are all critical to determining model impact.

The major conclusions of typical model validation studies and the types of data used to make these interpretations are shown in Table 8–4.

The validation of a design and development model, be it internal or external, is a summary judgment that emanates from a series of narrower conclusions pertaining to parts of the model. The broader interpretations of the data are often made with reservations or caveats. Researchers need to be especially cognizant of the intricacies and implications of their validation datasets.

Understanding Model Use Findings

Model researchers are usually aware of the constraints under which designers work. They know that in the "real world" good design and development models, even empirically validated models, are not always easy to use under some circumstances. Consequently, researchers interested in model use seek to find empirical answers to the following questions:

• What are the procedures that should be followed when using a particular model?

- Which conditions promote successful use of the model?
- How do you explain the successes or failures that can occur when using the model?

These are the major types of conclusions emanating from model use research.

These conclusions are dependent upon three types of data: project and participant profile data, context descriptions, and performance data. These data tend to be either exploratory or descriptive in nature.

The profile data provides descriptions of the projects undertaken and the participants in the design and development task. A dominant part of this literature addresses the impact of designer expertise on model use. Much of this research can be viewed as model use research. It is an important and expanding area of inquiry in the field.

Researchers are also currently concerned with the role of different settings on the use of a given model. These issues are addressed through the use of context data. The contextual ramifications of the design and development process have been highlighted in performance-improvement literature as well as constructivist thinking. These two areas of research—the role of context and expertise—are now leading to more realistic understandings of how design and development occurs. This is an important function of the findings of model use research.

The performance descriptions of designers, clients, and SMEs also serve as the basis of model use conclusions. These data inform us not only of how people follow a model, but also of the successes and failures they experience. Analyses of these experiences, both positive and negative, serve as the basis of valuable lessons for others. Failure data can be especially useful, even though many are reluctant to report such information. The explanations that researchers should provide are the reasons for the successes and failures and the extent to which they can be attributed to the model or to other factors in the environment.

The major conclusions of model use studies in the literature and the types of data that lead to these conclusions are shown in Table 8–5.

The process of drawing conclusions and interpreting a dataset is fraught with challenges. Some of these challenges can be met by using sound research skills, but others are less clear-cut. In the next section we will address two concerns that design and development researchers can face.

INTERPRETATION ISSUES

When researchers deal with data from natural work environments, they often encounter complications not faced by those working in laboratories or simu-

TABLE 8–5.
Model Use Conclusions and Supporting Data

Major Types of Conclusions Drawn	Key Types of Supporting Data
• Recommended procedures for model use • Conditions that promote successful model use • Explanations of successes or failures of model use	• Project Profile (e.g., scope, resource available) • Participant Profiles (e.g., designer/developers, clients, SMEs) • Design and Development Environment (e.g., parent organization, design organization characteristics) • In-Progress or Retrospective Data (e.g., designer/developer performance, problems & attitudes, client tasks & attitudes, SME tasks)

lated environments. We have discussed this issue with respect to data collection, but there are also ramifications for data interpretation. Here we will discuss two particular issues:

- Generalizing from project-specific data.
- Dealing with organizational concerns.

Generalizations and Project-Specific Data

There are two key issues that arise when researchers deal with project-specific data. One comes with data from single projects and the other with multi-project data. The single project issue concerns representation. Some design and development process recommendations (whether they are for products and tools or for general design models) spring from data from a single project. The dilemma is how illustrative this project is of those generally encountered in the workplace. If it is typical (and data can be presented to support this proposition), then the conclusions drawn from it can be meaningful for a wider range of projects.

Qualitative researchers argue that case-study data, such as those describing single projects, can often provide explanations superior to those based upon data from a broad population of participants. They reason that case-study data can allow researchers to delve more deeply into the topic. With respect to designer performances, for example, single-project data can help us learn more about the precise nature of the performances and the rationale for the performances than would be typically possible when collecting data from many sources. This is an argument favoring especially rich datasets over especially representative datasets (George & Bennett, 2005). You will need to analyze your conclusions and interpretations in light of these considerations to determine the extent of their applicability.

On the other hand, researchers informed by data from multiple projects have a different problem. The more projects (and, often, the more corresponding settings) that are addressed in a given study, the more likely the data will be broadly representative of the field. With this situation, it may be possible to identify common designer performances, for example, that are present across projects. The higher the frequency of similar types of designer performances, the greater the rationale for recommending their inclusion in models or sets of procedures.

The difficulty lies in determining the importance that should be given to outlier data. Are these more isolated performances aberrant behaviors or do they represent a typical response to a set of somewhat unusual, but not entirely unexpected, conditions? For example, when Adamski (1998) was validating the use of his job performance aid (JPA) design model he conducted a controlled flight simulation to test crew reactions in an emergency situation. In one performance measure, five of the six persons in the control group working without the JPA scored at the lowest level. The remaining person scored quite high working without the JPA. Should the researcher rely on the mean performance score to draw conclusions, or further investigate the person with the unusual performance? Datasets such as these present the researcher with hard choices when they are trying to make accurate interpretations.

The outlier question can be viewed in some circumstances as a matter of making objective decisions when interpreting qualitative data. Berg (2004) suggests that in these cases objectivity is linked to the extent to which the findings can be replicated in other studies—a point that pertains to quantitative, as well as qualitative, research. This speaks to the need for researchers to conduct a series of design and development studies before generalizations can be made with any degree of certainty. This is as true of multiple-project research as it is on single-project studies.

The Impact of Organizational Concerns

The vast majority of design and development research pertains to projects that have occurred or are occurring in natural work environments. While this lends an atmosphere of authenticity and practicality to the research, it can also introduce extraneous problems into the research process. Researchers must be cognizant (often they have no option) of the political implications of their findings for not only the organization, but also for those who have participated in the research. This issue becomes especially important when the find-ings are published.

Prior to the start of any research project, organizations and individuals agree to participate, and efforts are made to ensure that they are aware of what is involved. Nonetheless, it is not unusual in the course of a study for researchers to collect data of a sensitive nature that may create difficult situations for some participants. Perhaps the data are of a proprietary nature. Perhaps the data describe a design and development failure that occurred. Perhaps it is evalua-tive data that are not totally positive. Even though anonymity and confiden-tiality have been assured, people can still become concerned. Researchers are then confronted by the political implications of their findings.

We have stressed the importance of gathering contextual data. However, what if such data show performance in one manufacturing plant was clearly substandard? Even though actual plant names are not being reported, the researcher is likely to face great pressure from management to reveal the poorly performing plant so that remedies can be made. What should the researcher do? This is an actual situation that occurred in the course of a research project.

Clearly, organizations cannot dictate either the interpretation of findings or how they are reported, but they can expect all sides of a situation to be reported and the findings to be interpreted in light of organizational con-straints. Individuals have similar expectations. Researchers must be indepen-dent, yet still sensitive to the pressures felt by those in the workplace.

LOOKING AHEAD

This chapter has dealt with using design and development data to draw con-clusions and make interpretations. This process is typically intertwined with report writing. It is one of the most difficult phases of the research process, but probably the most important part. On the next page we provide a checklist of steps that can assist you in completing this task. Since interpretation is largely a matter of reflection, this checklist suggests the range of topics that should be addressed in this thinking process.

Now that the research process is drawing to a close, scholars often pause, look back, and answer the "So what?" questions. They think about what they have added to the field, and see all that is left to do. It is here that scholars also look to the future to determine how they will continue pursuing their larger research agendas.

We will also look to the future in the next chapter. There we will look at the expanding role of design and development research in the field, the varying approaches being taken with this type of research, and the emerging opportu-nities that exist for doing design and development research.

A CHECKLIST FOR INTERPRETING FINDINGS OF DESIGN AND DEVELOPMENT RESEARCH

1. Describe how findings from your design and development study can be used to expand the knowledge base of the field by asking the following questions:
   - How can the findings inform practice in the field?
   - How can the findings inform the theory of the field?
   - How can the findings expand the literature of the field?
   - How can the findings be used to generate new research questions?
2. Determine the "lessons learned" from your product or tool study by asking the following questions:
   - What processes can be recommended for the successful design and development of a similar product or tool?
   - Which conditions contribute to efficient design and development of the product or tool?
   - What procedures can be recommended for the successful use of a similar product or tool?
   - Which conditions promote successful use of the product or tool?
   - What is the impact of the product or tool?
   - Which conditions promote positive impact of the product or tool?
   - What suggestions can be made to improve the product or tool?
3. Determine the implications of your model development, validation or use study to by asking the following questions:
   - How can the findings be used to create a new or an enhanced model?
   - How do the findings confirm the model's components and their sequence?
   - How do the findings confirm the impact of the model?
   - What procedures can be suggested for the successful use of the model?
   - Which conditions promote successful use of the model?
   - How can the findings explain the successes or failures of the model?
4. Determine the generalizability of findings by examining your data and the research design used in your study.
5. Be sensitive to participants and the organization when interpreting and reporting findings from natural work environments.

9

The Status and
Future of Design and
Development Research

Educational research has always been viewed as a broad spectrum of inquiry encompassing both basic and applied topics. As early as 1964, Hilgard saw applied educational research as including the advocacy and adoption stages of technological development. As instructional systems design procedures became established, Baker (1973) explored the notion of instructional development as a scholarly activity. She noted that then product development was being seen by many as a type of applied research; thus, research and development were interrelated activities.

In this book, we have been exploring design and development not as an activity linked to research (even though it obviously is), but as an *object* of research. We have moved beyond the emphasis (that Baker noted in 1973) of ISD's use of evaluation data to using data to produce knowledge of the various design and development processes. In a sense, our analyses of design and development research have been an attempt to operationalize the relationships between research and development.

Clearly, we see design and development research as a critical part of IDT inquiry—one that needs to be expanded, improved, and refined. This chapter will explore the:

- Manner in which design and development research is expanding.
- Conditions that will facilitate future research.

THE EXPANSION OF DESIGN
AND DEVELOPMENT RESEARCH

Design and development research, as we have discussed it here, is expanding. More persons are tackling design problems from this research perspective. New models are being devised and validated. New products and programs are being empirically studied. In addition, other researchers are using alternative approaches to those discussed here to address many of the same problems. All of these research efforts highlight the importance of including design and development in the research process.

Alternative Approaches to Design and Development Research

Often different innovative approaches to solving a given problem emerge at roughly the same time. This is also true with respect to design and development research. The fact that different approaches have emerged speaks to a gap in our research that is apparently recognized fairly broadly. Two approaches will be discussed here:

1. Design-based research
2. Formative research

Design-based research.   Today, there is a growing allegiance to the tenets of design-based research or design experiments (Brown, 1992; Collins, 1992; Reeves, 2005). This is the study of learning in context (Design-Based Research Collective, 2003). Using this approach:

> designers build tools that they test in real classrooms and gather data that contribute both to the construction of theory and to the improvement of the tools. This process proceeds iteratively, over a period of time, until the tool is proven to be effective and our knowledge of why it is effective has been acquired and assimilated in theory. (Winn, 2004, p. 104)

Design-based research seeks to clarify the nature of the process by which people learn, typically through their interactions with instructional materials and other learners. This type of research design has been extensively used in the study of technology-based instructional materials. It is typically context-specific and to a great extent responds to those who challenge "the research community to conduct research that resides in and better supports classroom practice" (Sloane & Gorard, 2003, p. 30).

One example of a design-based study is Nelson, Ketelhut, Clarke, Bowman, and Dede (2005). This study involved the development of a graphical, multi-user virtual environment for use by middle-school students. It was designed to promote motivation and learning about science. This product was used in two public school classrooms, and the researchers went through four try-out/data collection/revision cycles. In the process, they were making discoveries about the effectiveness of learning theories as they were represented in their product.

Wang and Hannafin (2005) described how design-based methods are applied to technology-related research. They viewed this research as a combination of product research (i.e., the previous Type 1 developmental research) and model research (i.e., Type 2 research). They suggested that this combination occurs since their goals focus on the development of a specific product, but they also sought to identify more generalized design frameworks at the same time.

The Wang and Hannafin orientation, however, is somewhat different than most design-based research. The Design-Based Research Collective (2003) stated that this research is for "the study of learning in context through the systematic design and study of instructional strategies and tools" (p. 5). As such, many design experiments tend to be a type of teaching-learning research that relies upon an iterative formative evaluation process. It is often a form of context-specific research that informs designers of particular strategies that have proven to be effective ways of applying various learning theories. They do not necessarily speak to the design and development processes themselves, or to the development of design theory or principles, as do Wang and Hannafin (2005). Design-based research efforts, however, are innovative forms of inquiry that incorporate product development into the research process.

Formative research. Design and development research tactics can be applied to problems of a more theoretical nature even as they were applied to problems emerging from practical dilemmas. Reigeluth and Frick (1999) suggest the use of formative research techniques, a type of design and development research, as a way of testing existing design theories or providing the basis for the construction of a new theory or model. They propose that the products stemming from design theories be tested in terms of their effectiveness, their efficiency, and their appeal.

Existing theories can be tested by designing a product that is offered as an "instance" of the theory, and then collecting and analyzing formative data on this product. The product is revised and the data collection and revision cycle is repeated, resulting in corresponding revisions being made in the original theory. New theories can be developed through retrospective analysis of the design-data collection-revision process (Reigeluth & Frick, 1999).

There are similarities between the iterative revision cycles of formative research and design-based research; however, formative research specifically links theory formation or theory improvement to the research process. Design-based research efforts, on the other hand, tend to be more concerned with perfecting the teaching-learning processes stemming from learning theory. While not as commonly used as design-based research, formative research represents another approach to studying design processes. Moreover, it can not only refine the field's theory base, but can also highlight the validity and usefulness of theory-based techniques.

New Opportunities for Design and Development Research

Ultimately, the expansion of design and development research will depend more on the pressure exerted by critical disciplinary and workplace problems than the voices of advocates of this type of research. In Chapter 2, we discussed likely sources of problems consistent with design and development research: emerging technology, the workplace, and theory. We believe that these same problem areas will continue to stimulate this research in the future, probably in this order of magnitude. We will now discuss some ways these areas are likely to spawn new applications of design and development research techniques.

Exploration of new technologies. Through the years, technological advancements have stimulated much design and development research, especially product research. There are early examples of design and development studies that address instructional television (Albero-Andres, 1983; Cambre, 1979), interactive videodiscs (Alessi, 1988; Aukerman, 1987), and the use of hypertext (Harris & Cady, 1988). More recent design and development research has been conducted on newer technologies, such as automated design productivity tools (Gustafson & Reeves, 1990; Spector & Song, 1995). This pattern of researchers studying the emerging technologies using design and development strategies is likely to continue.

Of special interest now is the research related to technology-enhanced learning environments (TELEs). Wang and Hannafin (2005) define TELEs as "technology-based learning and instructional systems through which students acquire skills or knowledge, usually with the help of teachers or facilitators, learning support tools, and technological resourses" (p. 5). Through their research, they are able to reliably predict the effectiveness of the TELE tools, models, and principles. This is one example of cutting-edge technology systems that are being developed and studied using a type of design and development methodology.

Technology-oriented research, however, need not be directed only to instructional situations. Design and development research is appropriate for a variety of non-instructional topics and problems, using the same methodologies and strategies. It is likely that non-instructional interventions and tools will be a growing area of design and development research.

For example, there is a growing interest in performance improvement tools and systems, such as electronic-performance support systems (EPSS). Raybould (1995) defined an EPSS as "the electronic infrastructure that captures, stores and distributes individual and corporate knowledge assets throughout an organization, to enable individuals to achieve required levels of performance in the fastest possible time and with a minimum of support from other people" (p. 11). Over the years, various forms of tools that aim to improve workplace performance, rather than promote individual learning, have been developed. The development of these and other similar non-instructional tools are perfect objects of future design and development research projects.

Exploration of new workplace issues.   We have discussed the critical role of context and setting on design and development tasks, as well as on design and development research. The typical setting is in a workplace, or at times, workplace simulations. Workplace conditions and practitioner problems are not likely to disappear and those that do exist will continue to fuel new research efforts. Again, these problems will not be confined to traditional education and training settings. The design, development, and implementation of non-instructional interventions will be prominent, and research that does address instruction and learning may not always relate to individuals. Instead, they are likely to encompass organizational learning and group learning as well.

However, there are general setting issues that can be addressed (and hopefully will be addressed) by design and development researchers. For example, much of the IDT literature assumes that the fundamental principles of design and development can be generalized across settings and across content areas, even though we are becoming increasingly aware of the powerful impact of context on a project. These dichotomous positions point to another direction for future design and development research. Research that directly tackles time-honored tradition is more likely to occur given the growing diversity of researchers and of theoretical orientations.

What specific issues are likely to be addressed? One of the obvious sources of this new type of research pertains to studies of instructional design and development as it occurs in school settings. While a great deal of design and development research pertains to instructional products for use in schools, there is a paucity of research on the designer activity in schools. Young, Reiser, and Dick (1998) earlier approached this topic and interviewed award winning teachers to identify the general design tasks that they typically performed. Research such as this could also be directed toward specific types of design, such as designing for technology integration. Other studies are also needed to determine the extent to which design principles relate to specific settings. Not only school settings are important, but also, there is a rapidly expanding amount of activity in other settings, such as community-based education.

Exploration of new theory. Technology is a fairly straightforward impetus for design and development research, and this research is often prompted by clear-cut practitioner problems. Similarly, workplace problems demand resolution, and researchers respond. This typically is not the case with theory-related research. Ultimately, the idiosyncratic interests of individual scholars generate theory-based research.

Today's theories, especially with respect to IDT, are explored in the literature and then serve as the basis for innovative applications. They are more likely to result from theorizing and hypothesis generation than from an extended pattern of replicated research. This tends to be true of a wide variety of new theories. Design and development research is one way to inject systematic inquiry into the theory development process. It provides a mechanism for studying the applications of the various theoretical orientations, or to begin the process of validating the theories themselves.

Both types of design and development research lend themselves to this task. Product research can be conducted to show the exact way in which products reflecting a given theory are developed. The literature has many fine examples of detailed descriptions of theory-related products. Corno and Randi (1999), for example, provide a summary of research and theory pertaining to self-regulated learning. They then proceed to describe how these principles were applied to a high-school Latin course. This is not, however, design and development research.

Product research generated by theory consists of the systematic study of how products reflecting a given theory are developed and used. The impact of the products on learning or performance is also often studied. This type of research is somewhat akin to formative research with its emphasis on theory. One example of a study of this type is Gilbert and Driscoll (2002). This is a case study in which they designed a course based upon selected constructivist principles. They then tried out the course, testing the use of these principles. Finally, they proposed a set of guidelines for the design of collaborative, knowledge-building environments.

Model research can also be used to study the dimensions of a given theory. Studies of this type can produce general models of how to design and develop products that reflect the theory. Tracey and Richey's (in press) research resulted in an empirically based design model that was rooted in Gardner's (1993) theory of multiple intelligences. Another tactic would be to take an already constructed theory-based model, and conduct research to validate the model. For example, two such models are Willis's (1995) R2D2 constructivist model and van Merrienboer's cognitive 4C/ID model (van Merrienboer & Dijkstra, 1997). These are both prime targets for model validation research. Even though this research may not appear pressing from a practitioner orientation, it is likely to continue (and hopefully flourish) because of the interests and dedication of scholars in the field.

CONDITIONS THAT FACILITATE DESIGN AND DEVELOPMENT RESEARCH

What does it take for a field to make a new research technique commonplace? To some extent, this is a question of diffusion and dissemination, an issue that permeates many parts of the IDT field. It is also a function of capability and support. Researchers have identified those conditions that facilitate the adoption of innovations (Surry & Ely, 2002). Ely's (1990) studies have identified eight conditions. Those that are most applicable to implementing new research techniques are (a) dissatisfaction with the status quo, (b) knowledge of the innovation, and (c) availability of resources. We will explore each of these facets of the issue.

Dissatisfaction with Existing Research Orientations

Why would experienced researchers become dissatisfied with the traditional approaches to inquiry? Qualitative and quantitative research techniques have been well documented and offer opportunities to address a wide range of researchable problems. In the field of IDT, studies of teaching and learning continue to provide a firm foundation for much of the design and development knowledge base. We have discussed this in Chapter 1. There are problems, however, that scholars are beginning to recognize, including the following:

- The knowledge base pertaining to the designer and the design processes is not adequately informed by traditional research.
- Existing research does not routinely speak to the realities of design and development in the workplace.

Design and development research provides a way of addressing these problems and still use the many well-honed research strategies within our collective repertoires. Use, however, is dependent upon the prerequisite knowledge and skill, as well as a faith in the techniques.

Knowledge of the Innovation

Future researchers must first become aware of the fundamental nature of design and development research. A colleague of ours spoke to a small group of doctoral students who were not in an IDT program. In her presentation, she introduced them to design and development research techniques, and how they could be used to address a wide variety of problems characteristic of many content areas. Two persons from this group are now using this approach in their dissertation research. For example, a student in an educational leadership program was interested in proposing a dissertation that pertained to creating and implementing a professional development program for teachers. Design and development techniques applied perfectly to his problem, and upon introduction to it, he saw its utility and became a "convert" immediately.

Advocacy, however, is not enough. Competent design and development researchers must have not only all of the fundamental research skills, but they must be knowledgeable in the strategies that can be employed to address the unique problems one is confronted with in these types of studies. Furthermore, they must be able to design the studies so that many of these problems can be avoided altogether. Many will develop these skills through experience. Others will be taught them in their graduate programs, but future use of these techniques is clearly dependent upon some degree of professional development in the field.

Availability of Resources

Not surprisingly, the third requirement for adopting these new techniques relates to resources. One of the most important resources for much design and development research is a source of data, and typically this involves the support of an organization involved in design and development projects. Collaborative partnerships between academe and the workplace can produce knowledge that is relevant and useful to practitioners and theorists alike. In the past, these have arisen out of personal relationships to a great extent. Students also can create bridges between universities and their workplaces, and more formal relationships have been established between schools, businesses, and research institutes. Whatever path is taken, these links are vital to many high-quality design and development research projects.

In Chapter 7, we discussed plans and uses of design and development research laboratories. These facilities add to the range of studies that can be conducted. They can be extensive, fully equipped, and connected to other facilities at remote locations, or they can be fairly modest in design, as we discussed earlier. All research universities should consider them as an avenue to expanding the research agendas of faculty and students. In addition, many private corporations are building such facilities to test product usability.

Finally, most researchers think first of how to secure the financial support necessary for their projects. At this point in time, few funding agencies are specifically calling for design and development research in their requests for proposals. While this is not likely to occur soon, it should be possible for researchers to become change agents by building design and development research into their funding proposals, and thus educating these agencies in this alternative research path.

Of most help to researchers would be more organizations that fund design and development studies. While traditional government and foundation sources will continue to support school-based research, we need a more extensive array of organizations that fund research in the private sector. This is not uncommon with respect to engineering research. Corporate funding of design and development research could provide these same organizations with findings that could substantially reduce their costs.

CONCLUSIONS

This book has been about how to plan and conduct design and development research. It has provided you with detailed direction for each part of the research process. In addition, it has given you a wealth of examples from actual design and development studies—problems addressed, research designs, populations included in studies, data collection instruments and procedures, and ways of interpreting your findings. Interwoven among these details, however, we have been (not too subtly) advocating and promoting the use of these strategies to address what we feel are critical needs of the IDT field.

Ultimately, our goal is to see a proliferation of design and development research. We would like to see our journals filled with empirical research on design and development, rather than simply discussion pieces. We would like to see practitioners demand data to support the planned use of design and development tactics. We would like to see our theory being supported by a firm empirical foundation. Most of all we would like researchers to be able to provide practical, substantiated solutions to the problems confronted by those working in the design and development field.

Glossary of Terms

Applied Research—Systematic empirical inquiry directed toward providing information to solve existing problems (see Singleton & Straits, 2005).

Case Study—An in-depth investigation of an individual, group, or institution to determine the variables, and the relationship among the variables, influencing the current behavior or status of the subject of the study (Wallen & Fraenkel, 2001, p. 515).

Causal Inference—A logically derived causal explanation of the phenomena studied (see King, Keohane, & Verba, 1994).

Cause—A factor that helps to bring about the occurrence of an outcome (Brady & Collier, 2004, p. 278).

Component Investigation—A study of the elements of a design and development model; a form of internal model validation.

Conceptual Model—Models that define, explain, and describe relationships among variables; they can have a variety of formats, such as narrative descriptions, taxonomies, mathematical formulations, or visualizations (Richey, 1986).

Confirmative Evaluation—A type of evaluation that "goes beyond formative and summative evaluation to judge the continued merit, value, or worth of a long-term training program" (Dessinger & Moseley, 2004, p. 204).

Constructivism—A school of psychology which holds that learning occurs because personal knowledge is constructed by an active and self-regulated learner who solves problems by deriving meaning from experience and the context in which that experience takes place (Seels & Richey, 1994, p. 127).

Context Data—Information pertaining to the setting and environment in which design and development occurs, in which the intervention is implemented, or in which the skills and knowledge are applied.

Contextual Analysis—A systematic process of identifying the critical elements of a design and development setting or environment (see "context data").

Content Analysis—The process of inductively establishing a categorical system for organizing open-ended information (Wallen & Fraenkel, 2001, p. 516); commonly used in qualitative research.

Controlled Testing—An experiment that isolates the effects of a model or compares them to the effects of other models or approaches; a form of external model validation.

Correlation—A measure of the association between two or more variables (Brady & Collier, 2004, p. 282).

Critical Incident Technique—Procedures for collecting observed incidents having special significance and meeting systematically defined criteria (Flanagan, 1988, p. 277); used to collect retrospective data on the behaviors that contribute to success or failure in specific situations.

Cycle Time—The amount of time required to complete a design and development project using predetermined starting and ending events; may be elapsed time or actual work time.

Daily Log—See "work log."

Data—Information collected by a researcher, typically organized for analysis and used as a basis for inference (Brady & Collier, 2004, p. 283).

Data Collection Instrument—A device used to gather information that will facilitate the description and measurement of variables; commonly includes items such as surveys, tests, observation guides, checklists, rating scales, and interview protocols.

Data Collection Tool—See "data collection instrument."

Dataset—A collection of quantitative or qualitative information pertaining to one or more variables across a given set of cases (see Brady & Collier, 2004).

Delphi Research Methods—A technique used to elicit opinion and seek consensus of a group of experts; begins with an open-ended questionnaire and is followed by a series of rounds in which participants respond to the questionnaire and the responses of others.

Demographic Data—Statistical descriptions of a population or a sample.

Dependent Variable—What the researcher seeks to explain. It is hypothesized to be caused by, or be "dependent" on, one or more independent variables (Brady & Collier, 2004, p. 284).

Descriptive Research—A qualitative or quantitative study that is a "fact-finding enterprise, focusing on relatively few dimensions of a well-defined entity" (Singleton & Straits, 2005, p. 68).

Design—The process of specifying conditions for learning (Seels & Richey, 1994, p. 127).

Design and Development Research—The systematic study of design, development, and evaluation processes with the aim of establishing an empirical basis for the creation of instructional and non-instructional products and tools and new or enhanced models that govern their development.

Design-Based Research—The study of learning in context through the systematic design and study of instructional strategies and tools (Design-Based Research Collective, 2003, p. 5).

Designer Characteristics—Those facets of the designer's profile and experiential background that may impact the design and development process.

Designer Decision-Making Research—Investigations of designer activities including designer problem-solving, thinking, and use of models; commonly includes explorations of the differences between novice and expert designers.

Development—The process of translating the design specifications into physical form (Seels & Richey, 1994, p. 127).

Development Research—See "design and development research."

Developmental Research—See "design and development research."

Empirical Research—Any type of research based on planned observation and evidence (see Brady & Collier, 2004, p. 286).

Evaluation Research—Research that gathers data for decision-making in order to prove, improve, expand, or discontinue a project or program (Seels & Richey, 1994, p. 128).

Experimental Research—Research in which at least one independent variable is manipulated, other relevant variables are controlled, and the effect on one or more dependent variables is observed (Wallen & Fraenkel, 2001, p. 517).

Expert Review Research Methods—A variety of data collection techniques designed to gather the opinions of subject matter experts on design and development models and products; a form of internal model validation.

Explanatory Research—Studies that describe phenomena and test relationships between the elements of a problem; tends to be quantitative research designed to "seek the answers to problems and hypotheses" (Singleton & Straits, 2005, p. 69).

Exploratory Research—Studies that relate to topics about which very little is known; tends to be qualitative research (Singleton & Straits, 2005).

Extant Data—Information derived from existing records or documents.

External Model Validation—The empirical verification of the impact of a product created using a design and development model.

Field Evaluation—See "field test"; also, a common form of external validation of design and development models.

Field Observation—On-site examination and collection of data pertaining to designers and developers, or the implementation of interventions, or the application of skills and knowledge.

Field Test—Tryout and formative evaluation of a program or product in the setting in which it is intended to be used; also known as "field trial" (see Dick, Carey, & Carey, 2005).

Focus Group—Unstructured discussions among a small group of participants, focused on a general topic and guided by a skilled interviewer (Singleton & Straits, 2005, p. 563).

Formative Evaluation—Gathering information on the adequacy of an instructional product or program and using this information as a basis for further development (Seels & Richey, 1994, p. 128); may also apply to non-instructional products.

Formative Research—A type of "developmental research . . . that is intended to improve design theory for designing instructional practices or processes" (Reigeluth & Frick, 1999, p. 633).

Generalization—The application of research findings to larger populations and different settings.

Hypothesis—An expected but unconfirmed relationship among two or more variables (Singleton & Straits, 2005, p. 563)

IDT—The field of instructional design and technology.

ISD—See "instructional systems design."

Independent Variable—A variable that influences, or is hypothesized to influence, the dependent variable (see Brady & Collier, 2004, p. 290).

In-Depth Interview—A focused, intensive data collection technique in which participants are questioned orally to elicit a detailed description of their perceptions and opinions.

Informed Consent—Agreement of an individual to be involved in a research project based upon explanations of the potential risks and consequences related to such participation.

In-Progress Project Data—Information collected during the course of a design and development project.

Institutional Review Board—A committee of researchers and community members who determine if the proposed research procedures protect the rights of human subjects.

Instructional Systems Design—An organized procedure for developing instructional materials or programs that includes the steps of analyzing (defining what is to be learned), designing (specifying how the learning should occur), developing (authoring or producing the material), implementing (using the materials or strategies in context), and evaluating (determining the adequacy of instruction) (Seels & Richey, 1994, p. 129).

Internal Model Validation—The empirical verification of the components and processes included in a design and development model.

Interpretation—The process of explaining and deriving meaning from data.

Interview Protocol—An open-ended questionnaire used in qualitative research to guide the oral questioning of participants.

Learner Characteristics—Those facets of the learner's experiential background that impact the effectiveness of a learning process (Seels & Richey, 1994, p. 130).

Learning Path—The sequence of activities that a learner selects and follows through an instructional product; commonly pertains to computer-mediated instruction.

Likert Scale—A technique designed to measure attitudes, typically using a continuum of "strongly agree" to "strongly disagree" (see Frankfort-Nachmias & Nachmias, 2000).

Mixed Methods Research—Studies that use a combination of quantitative and qualitative research methods.

Model Research—The study of the development, validation, and use of design and development models, leading primarily to generalized conclusions.

Multiple Methods Research—Studies that use a variety of similar research methods, either quantitative or qualitative.

Naturalistic Research—A form of qualitative research in which "the observer controls or manipulates nothing, and tries not to affect the observed situation in any way" (Wallen & Fraenkel, 2001, p. 520).

Needs Assessment—A systematic process for determining goals, identifying discrepancies between goals and the status quo, and establishing priorities for action (Briggs, 1977, p. xxiv).

Observation Guide—A planned data collection tool that enables researchers to gather information on behavior and performance as it occurs; guides may relate to either controlled or non-controlled observation systems (see Frankfort-Nachmais & Nachmias, 2000).

Operational Definition—The specification of "the actions or operations required to measure or identify the term" (Wallen & Frankel, 2001, p. 16).

Organizational Climate—The cultural and environmental characteristics of a given setting; often relates to factors such as goals and values, reward systems, leadership style, and group code.

Participants—The individuals from whom data are collected in a design and development research project; may include designers, developers, clients, instructors, or learners.

Performance Data—Information collected pertaining to human or organizational behavior and accomplishment.

Performance Improvement—A focus on improving individual, group, and organizational behavior and accomplishment through the use of a variety of interventions.

Procedural Models—Models that describe how to perform a task (see Richey, 1986).

Product and Tool Research—The study of specific product or tool design, development, or use projects leading primarily to context-specific conclusions; pertains to either comprehensive projects or specific project phases.

Profile Data—The information that describes the characteristics or provides a biographical sketch of participants or design and development projects; see also "demographic data."

Project Characteristics—Those facets of a project's profile, context, or participants that impact the operation of the project or the effectiveness of the resulting product.

Prototype—Workable models of a final product, or shells that demonstrate the projected appearance of a product (Jones & Richey, 2000).

Purposeful Sampling—Selecting participants and settings for inclusion in a study based upon the criteria of the study; commonly used in qualitative research (Rudestam and Newton, 2001).

Qualitative Research—An approach to scientific inquiry which typically uses non-experimental methods, such as ethnography or case history, to study important variables that are not easily manipulated or controlled, and which emphasizes using multiple methods for collecting, recording, and analyzing data rather than using statistical analysis (Seels & Richey, 1994, p. 133).

Quantitative Research—An approach to scientific investigation that typically "employs strategies of inquiry such as experiments and surveys, and collects data on predetermined instruments that yield statistical data" (Creswell, 2003, p. 18).

Random Sampling—A method of selecting participants in which every accessible member of a population has an equal chance of being chosen.

Rapid Prototyping—An instructional design methodology in which designers work with clients to quickly build a series of prototypes for instruction in order to experiment with and evaluate a variety of instructional designs before committing to a single instructional approach for further development (Bichelmeyer, 2004, p. 483).

Recall Data—See "retrospective data."

Research Design—The program that guides the investigator in the process of collecting, analyzing, and interpreting observations (Frankfort-Nachmias & Nachmias, 2000, p. 597).

Retrospective Data—Information collected about a design and development project after it has been completed.

Rubric—An instrument used for making a general assessment of a product or performance that gives a descriptive, holistic characterization of the quality of the product or performance (see Morrison, Ross, & Kemp, 2006).

Screen Capture—A copy of a computer screen's contents.

SME—Subject matter expert.

Summative Evaluation—Gathering information on the effectiveness of an instructional or non-instructional intervention to make determinations of the worth of the intervention or make recommendations about its retention.

Survey Research—An attempt to obtain data from members of a population (or a sample) to determine the current status of that population with respect to one or more variables (Wallen & Fraenkel, 2001, p. 523).

Task Analysis—A process used to determine how a task is performed and to identify the attributes that affect performance (Wolfe, Wetzel, Harris, Mazour, & Riplinger, 1991, p. 170).

Theory—A set of related propositions that attempts to explain, and sometimes to predict, a set of events (Hoover & Donovan, 1995, p. 69).

Think-Aloud Methods—A research strategy in which participants describe out loud what they are thinking while carrying out a task.

Time-on-Task—The amount of time spent working on a given activity, not the total elapsed time since the start of that activity.

Triangulation—Cross-checking of data using multiple data sources or multiple data-collection procedures (Wallen & Fraenkel, 2001, p. 523); commonly used in qualitative research.

Tryout Data—Information collected pertaining to the use and/or effectiveness of an instructional or non-instructional product or program.

Type 1 Developmental Research—See "product and tool research."

Type 2 Developmental Research—See "model research."

Usability Documentation—Information on the extent to which a product, tool, or model can be effectively, efficiently, and satisfactorily used in the context for which it was intended; a common form of internal validation of design and development models (see Norton, 2004a).

Variable—A concept that has degrees of difference in quantity or quality; is thought to influence, or be influenced by, something else; see also "dependent variable" and "independent variable."

Web-Based Survey—Self-administered data collection instruments that participants complete while using the World Wide Web (Norton, 2004b, p. 644).

Work Log—An instrument used to collect data such as designer activities, resources, reactions, and time-on-task.

Work Sample—Documents from completed or in-progress design and development projects that are representative of the various project stages, products, and decisions made; see also "extant data."

References

Adamski, A. J. (1998). The development of a systems design model for job performance aids: A qualitative developmental study (Doctoral dissertation, Wayne State University, 1998). *Dissertation Abstracts International-A, 59*(03), 789.

Albero-Andres, M. (1983). The use of the Agency for Instructional Television instructional development model in the design, production, and evaluation of the series of Give and Take (Doctoral dissertation, Indiana University, 1982). *Dissertation Abstracts International-A, 43*(11), 3489.

Alessi, S. M. (1988). Learning interactive videodisc development: A case study. *Journal of Instructional Development, 11*(2), 2–7.

Armstrong, A. (2003). *Instructional design in the real world: A view from the trenches.* Hershey, PA: The Idea Group.

Aukerman, M. E. (1987). Effectiveness of an interactive video approach for CPR recertification of registered nurses (Doctoral dissertation, University of Pittsburgh, 1986). *Dissertation Abstracts International-A, 47*(06), 1979.

Baker, E. L. (1973). The technology of instructional development. In R. M. W. Travers (Ed.), *Second handbook of research on teaching* (pp. 245–285). Chicago: Rand McNally & Company.

Banathy, B. H. (1968). *Instructional systems.* Palo Alto, CA: Fearon Publishers.

Beauchamp, M. (1991). The validation of an integrative model of student affect variables and instructional systems design (Doctoral dissertation, Wayne State University, 1990). *Dissertation Abstracts International-A, 51*(6), 1885.

Berg, B. L. (2004). *Qualitative research methods for the social sciences* (5th ed.). Boston, MA: Pearson Education, Inc.

Bichelmeyer, B. (2004). Rapid prototyping. In A. Kovalchick & K. Dawson (Eds.), *Education and technology: An encyclopedia, Volume 2:J-Z* (pp. 483–489). Santa Barbara, CA: ABC CLIO.

Bracht, G. H., & Glass, G. V. (1968). The external validity of experiments. *American Educational Research Journal, 5,* 437–474.

Brady, H. E., & Collier, D. (Eds.). (2004). *Rethinking social inquiry: Diverse tools, shared standards.* Lanham, MD: Rowman & Littlefield Publishers, Inc.

Brewer, J., & Hunter, A. (2006). *Foundations of multimethod research: Synthesizing styles.* Thousand Oaks, CA: Sage Publications.

Briggs, L. J. (Ed.). (1977). *Instructional design: Principles and applications.* Englewood Cliffs, NJ: Educational Technology Publications.

Broderick, M. (1963). Logic and scientific method in research on teaching. In N. L. Gage (Ed.), *Handbook of research on teaching* (pp. 44–93). Chicago: Rand McNally & Company.

Brolin, R. M., Milheim, W. D., & Viechnicki, K. J. (1993–94). The development of a model for the design of motivational adult instruction in higher education. *Journal of Educational Technology Systems, 22*(1), 3–17.

Brown, A. L. (1992). Design experiments: Theoretical and methodological challenges in creating complex interventions in classroom settings. *Journal of the Learning Sciences, 2,* 141–178.

Cambre, M. A. (1979). The development of formative evaluation procedures for instructional film and television: The first fifty years (Doctoral dissertation, Indiana University, 1978). *Dissertation Abstracts International-A, 39*(7), 3995.

Campbell, D. T., & Stanley, J. C. (1963). Experimental and quasi-experimental designs for research. In N. L. Gage (Ed.), *Handbook of research on teaching* (pp. 171–246). Chicago: Rand McNally & Company.

Carliner, S. (1998). How designers make decisions: A descriptive model of instructional design for informal learning in museums. *Performance Improvement Quarterly, 11*(2), 72–92.

Carr-Chellman, A., Cuyar, C., & Breman, J. (1998). User-design: A case application in health care training. *Educational Technology Research and Development, 46*(4), 97–114.

Chase, C. A. (2003). The effects of gender differences and levels of expertise on instructional design (Doctoral dissertation, Wayne State University, 2002). *Dissertation Abstracts International-A, 63*(11), 3815.

Chomei, T., & Houlihan, R. (1970). Comparative effectiveness of three language laboratory methods using a new equipment system. *Audio-Visual Communication Review, 18*(2), 160–168.

Chou, C., & Sun C. (1996). Constructing a cooperative distance learning system: The CORAL experience. *Educational Technology Research and Development, 44*(4), 71–84.

Clark, R. E., & Estes, F. (1998). Technology or craft: What are we doing? *Educational Technology, 42*(5), 5–11.

Cobb, R.W., & Elder, C. D. (1983). *Participation in American politics: The dynamics of agenda-building* (2nd ed.). Baltimore, MD: The Johns Hopkins University Press.

Cochran, W. (1977). *Sampling techniques* (3rd ed.). New York: John Wiley & Sons.

Collins, A. (1992). Toward a design science of education. In E. Scanlon & T. O'Shea (Eds.), *Issues in education research: Problems and possibilities.* San Francisco: Jossey-Bass.

Corno, L., & Randi, J. (1999). A design theory for classroom instruction in self-regulated learning? In C. M. Reigeluth (Ed.), *Instructional design theories and models, Volume II: A new paradigm of instructional theory* (pp. 293–318). Mahwah, NJ: Lawrence Erlbaum Associates, Publishers.

Corry, M. D., Frick, T. W., & Hansen, L. (1997). User-centered design and usability testing of a web site: An illustrative case study. *Educational Technology Research and Development, 45*(4), 65–76.

Cowell, D. M. (2001). Needs assessment activities and techniques of instructional designers: A qualitative study (Doctoral dissertation, Wayne State University, 2000). *Dissertation Abstracts International-A, 61*(10), 3873.

Creswell, J. W. (2003). *Research design: Qualitative, quantitative, and mixed methods approaches* (2nd ed.). Thousand Oakes, CA: Sage Publications.

Davies, I. K. (1981). Instructional development as an art: One of the three faces of ID. *Performance & Instruction, 20*(7), 4–7.

Design-Based Research Collective. (2003). Design-based research: An emerging paradigm for educational inquiry. *Educational Researcher, 32*(1), 5–8.

Dessinger, J. C., & Moseley, J. L. (2004). *Confirmative evaluation: Practical strategies for valuing continuous improvement.* San Francisco, CA: Pfeiffer, A Wiley Imprint.

Dick, W. (1981). Instructional design models: Future trends and issues. *Educational Technology, 21*(7), 29–32.

Dick, W. (1997). A model for the systematic design of instruction. In R. D. Tennyson, F. Schott, N. M. Seel & S. Dijkstra's (Eds.), *Instructional design: International perspectives: Volume 1—Theory, research and methods* (pp. 361–369). Mahwah, NJ.: Lawrence Erlbaum Associates, Publishers.

Dick, W., & Carey, L. (1996). *The systematic design of instruction* (4th ed). New York: Harper-Collins Publishers.

Dick, W., Carey, L., & Carey, J. O. (2005). *The systematic design of instruction* (6th ed.). New York: Allyn & Bacon/Longman Publishers.

Driscoll, M. P. (1984). Paradigms for research in instructional systems. *Journal of Instructional Development, 7*(4), 2–5.

Duffy, T. M., & Cunningham, D. J. (1996). Constructivism: Implications for the design and delivery of instruction. In D. Jonassen (Ed.), *Handbook of research for educational communications and technology* (pp. 170–198). Mahwah, NJ: Lawrence Erlbaum Associates, Publishers.

Edmonds, G. S., Branch, R. C., & Mukherjee, P. (1994). A conceptual framework for comparing instructional design models. *Educational Technology Research and Development, 42*(4), 55–72.

Elder, C. D., & Cobb, R.W. (1984). Agenda-building and the politics of aging. *Policy Studies Journal, 13*(1), 115–129.

Ely, D. (1990). Conditions that facilitate the implementation of educational technology innovations. *Journal of Research on Computing in Education, 23*(2), 298–305.

Ericsson, K. A. (2004). Deliberate practice and the acquisition and maintenance of expert performance in medicine and related domains. *Academic Medicine, 79*(10), 70–81.

Ericsson, K. A., & Charness, N. (1994). Expert performance: Its structure and acquisition. *American Psychologist, 49*(8), 725–747.

Finn, J. D. (1953). Professionalizing the audio-visual field. *Audio-Visual Communication Review, 1*(1), 6–17.

Fischer, K. M., Savenye, W. C., & Sullivan, H. J. (2002). Formative evaluation of computer-based training for a university financial system. *Performance Improvement Quarterly, 15*(1), 11–24.

Flanagan, J. C. (1988). The critical incident technique. In R. Zemke and T. Kramlinger's (Eds.), *Figuring things out: A trainer's guide to needs and task analysis* (pp. 277–317).

Reading, MA: Addison-Wesley Publishing Company, Inc. (Reprinted from *Psychological Bulletin*, v. 51 [July, 1954], pp. 327–58.)

Forsyth, J. E. (1998). The construction and validation of a model for the design of community-based train-the-trainer instruction (Doctoral dissertation, Wayne State University, 1997). *Dissertation Abstracts International-A, 58*(11), 4242.

Fowler, F. J. (2002). *Survey research methods* (3rd ed.). Thousand Oaks, CA: Sage Publications.

Fox, E. J., & Klein, J. D. (2003). What should instructional designers and technologists know about human performance technology? *Performance Improvement Quarterly, 16*(3), 87–98.

Foxon, M., Richey, R. C., Roberts, R., & Spannaus, T. (2003). *Training manager competencies: The standards* (3rd ed.). Syracuse, NY: ERIC Clearinghouse on Information and Technology.

Frankfort-Nachmias, C., & Nachmias, D. (2000). *Research methods in the social sciences* (6th ed.). New York: St. Marin's Press.

Freeman, P. (1983). Fundamentals of design. In P. Freeman (Ed.), *Software design tutorial* (pp. 2–22). New York: IEEE Computer Society Press.

Gagne, R. M. (1985). *The conditions of learning and theory of instruction* (4th ed.). New York: Holt, Rinehart and Winston.

Gagne, R. M., Wager, W. W., Golas, K. C., & Keller, J. M. (2005). *Principles of instructional design*. (4th ed.) Belmont, CA: Wadsworth/Thompson Learning.

Gall, M. D., Gall, J. P., & Borg, W. R. (2003). *Educational research: An introduction* (7th ed.). Boston: Allyn and Bacon.

Gardner, H. (1993). *Frames of mind: The theory of multiple intelligences*. New York: Basic Books.

Gay, G., & Mazur, J. (1993). The utility of computer tracking tools for user-centered design. *Educational Technology, 33*(4), 45–59.

George, A. L., & Bennett, A. (2005). *Case studies and theory development in the social sciences*. Cambridge, MA: MIT Press.

Gettman, D., McNelly, T., & Muraida, D. (1999). The guided approach to instructional design advising (GUIDA): A case-based approach to developing instructional design expertise. In J. van den Akker, R. M. Branch, K. Gustafson, N. Nieveen & T. Plomp's (Eds.), *Design approaches and tools in education and training* (pp. 175–182). Dordrecht, The Netherlands: Kluwer Academic Publishers.

Gilbert, N. J., & Driscoll, M. P. (2002). Collaborative knowledge building: A case study. *Educational Technology Research and Development, 50*(1), 59–79.

Greenhill, L. P. (1955). *A study of the feasibility of local production of minimum cost sound motion pictures*. (Pennsylvania State University Instructional Film Research Program). Port Washington, NY: US Naval Training Device Center, Office of Naval Research, Technical Report No. SDC 269-7-48.

Gustafson, K. L., & Branch, R. M. (2002). *Survey of instructional development models* (4th ed.). Syracuse, NY: ERIC Clearinghouse on Information & Technology.

Gustafson, K. L., & Reeves, T. C. (1990). IDioM: A platform for a course development expert system. *Educational Technology, 30*(3), 19–25.

Hallamon, T. C. (2002). A study of factors affecting the use of task analysis in the design of instruction (Doctoral dissertation, Wayne State University, 2001). *Dissertation Abstracts International-A, 62*(12), 4131.

Harris, M., & Cady, M. (1988). The dynamic process of creating hypertext literature. *Educational Technology, 28*(11), 33–40.

Heinich, R. (1984). The proper study of instructional technology. *Educational Communication and Technology Journal, 32*(2), 67–87.

Hilgard, E. R. (Ed.). (1964). *Theories of learning and instruction. The sixty-third yearbook of the National Society for the Study of Education.* Chicago: University of Chicago Press.

Higgins, N., & Reiser, R. (1985). Selecting media for instruction: An exploratory study. *Journal of Instructional Development, 8*(2), 6–10.

Hirumi, A., Savenye, W., & Allen, B. (1994). Designing interactive videodisc-based museum exhibits: A case study. *Educational Technology Research and Development, 42*(1), 47–55.

Hoban, C. F. (1953). Determinants of audience reaction to a training film. *Audio-Visual Communication Review, 1*(1), 30–37.

Hoover, K. R., & Donovan, T. (1995). *The elements of social scientific thinking* (6th ed.). Belmont, CA: Thompson/Wadsworth.

Johnson, R. B., & Onwuegbuzie, A. J. (2004). Mixed methods research: A research paradigm whose time has come. *Educational Researcher, 33*(7), 14–16.

Jonassen, D. H. (Ed.). (1996). *Handbook of research for educational communications and technology.* New York: Simon & Schuster Macmillan.

Jonassen, D. H. (Ed.). (2004). *Handbook of research for educational communications and technology* (2nd ed.). Mahwah, NJ: Lawrence Erlbaum Associates, Publishers.

Jones, T. S. (1999). Validating the process of designing and developing instructional materials using the rapid prototyping methodology (Doctoral dissertation, Wayne State University, 1998). *Dissertation Abstracts International-A, 59*(12), 4409.

Jones, T. S., & Richey, R. C. (2000). Rapid prototyping in action: A developmental study. *Educational Technology Research and Development, 48*(2), 63–80.

Kaner, J. H., & Rosenstein, A. J. (1960). Television in army training: Color vs. black and white. *Audio-Visual Communication Review, 8*(6), 243–252.

Keller, J. M. (1987). The systematic process of motivational design. *Performance & Instruction, 26*(10), 1–8.

King, G., Keohane, R. O., & Verba, S. (1994). *Designing social inquiry: Scientific inference in qualitative research.* Princeton, NJ: Princeton University Press.

Klein, J. D., Brinkerhoff, J., Koroghlanian, C., Brewer, S., Ku, H., & MacPherson-Coy, A. (2000). The foundations of educational technology: A needs assessment. *TechTrends, 44*(6), 32–36.

Klein, J. D., Nguyen, F., Bevill, L., Winter, C., Reisslein, J., & Fox, E. (2003, October). *Teaching performance improvement: Can we help clients identify and solve their problems?* Paper presented at the annual meeting of the Association for Educational Communications and Technology. Anaheim, CA.

Klein, J. D., & Rushby, N. (2007). Professional organizations and publications in instructional design and technology. In R. A. Reiser & J. V. Dempsey (Eds.), *Trends and issues in instructional design and technology* (2nd ed.) (pp. 260–270). Saddle River, NJ: Pearson Prentice Hall.

Klein, J. D., Spector, J. M., Grabowski, B., & de la Teja, I. (2004). *Instructor competencies: Standards for face-to-face, online, and blended settings.* Greenwich, CT: Information Age Publishing.

Koszalka, T. A. (2001). Designing synchronous distance education: A demonstration project. *The Quarterly Review of Distance Education, 2*(4), 333–345.

Krejcie, R. V., & Morgan, D. W. (1970). Determining sample size for research activities. *Educational and Psychological Measurement, 30,* 607–610.

Leedy, P. D. (1985). *Practical research: Planning and design* (3rd ed.). New York: Macmillan.

Le Maistre, C. (1998). What is an expert instructional designer? Evidence of expert performance during formative evaluation. *Educational Technology Research and Development, 46*(3), 21–36.

Levine, H. G. (1992). Naturalistic inquiry, types of. In M. C. Alkin (Ed.) *Encyclopedia of educational research* (6th ed.) (pp. 889–892). New York: Macmillan Publishing Company.

Li, Z., & Merrill, M. D. (1991). ID Expert 2.0: Design theory and process. *Educational Technology Research and Development, 39*(2), 53–69.

Link, N., & Cherow-O'Leary, R. (1990). Research and development of print materials at the Children's Television Workshop. *Educational Technology Research and Development, 38*(4), 34–44.

Littlejohn. S. W. (1978). *Theories of human communication.* Columbus, OH: Charles E. Merrill Publishing Company.

Luiz, T. (1983). A comparative study of humanism and pragmatism as they relate to decision making in instructional development processes (Doctoral dissertation, Michigan State University, 1982). *Dissertation Abstracts International-A, 43*(12), 3839.

Lumsdaine, A. A. (1953). Audio-visual research in the U.S. Air Force. *Audio-Visual Communication Review, 1*(2), 76–90.

Markle, S. M. (1967). Empirical testing of programs. In P. C. Lange (Ed.), *Programed instruction: The sixty-sixth yearbook of the National Society for the Study of Education, Part II* (pp. 104–138). Chicago: The University of Chicago Press.

Martin, B., & Bramble, W. (1996). Designing effective video teletraining instruction: The Florida teletraining project. *Educational Technology Research and Development, 44*(1), 85–99.

McCracken, G. (1988). *The long interview.* Newbury Park, CA: Sage Publications.

McKenney, S. (2002). Computer-based support for science education materials development in Africa: Exploring potentials (Doctoral dissertation, Universiteit Twente [The Netherlands], 2001). *Dissertation Abstracts International-C, 63*(03), 355.

McKenney, S., & van den Akker, J. (2005). Computer-based support for curriculum designers: A case of developmental research. *Educational Technology Research and Development, 53*(2), 41–66.

McLellan, H. (2004). Virtual realities. In D. Jonassen (Ed.), *Handbook of research for educational communications and technology* (2nd ed.) (pp. 461–498). Mahwah, NJ: Lawrence Erlbaum Associates, Publishers.

Means, T. B., Jonassen, D. H., & Dwyer, F. M. (1997). Enhancing relevance: Embedded ARCS strategies vs. purpose. *Educational Technology Research and Development, 45*(1), 5–17.

Medley, D. M. (1992). Structured observation. In M. C. Alkin (Ed.), *Encyclopedia of educational research* (6th Ed.) (pp. 1310–1315). New York: Macmillan Publishing Company.

Merrill, M. D. (1983). Component display theory. In C. Reigeluth (Ed.), *Instructional-design theories and models: An overview of their current status* (pp. 279–333). Hillsdale, NJ: Lawrence Erlbaum Associates, Publishers.

Merrill, M. D., Drake, L., Lacy, M. J., Pratt, J. A., & the ID2 Research Group. (1996). Reclaiming instructional design. *Educational Technology, 36*(5), 5–7.

Merrill, M. D., & Li, Z. (1989). An instructional design expert system. *Journal of Computer-Based Instruction, 16*(3), 95–101.

Milrad, M., Spector, J. M., & Davidsen, P. I. (2000). Building and using simulation based environments for learning about complex domains. In R. Robson (Ed.), *MSET/2000 conference proceedings* (pp. 304–308). Charlottesville, VA: Association for the Advancement of Computing in Education.

Mooij, T. (2002). Designing a digital instructional management system to optimize early education. *Educational Technology Research and Development, 50*(4), 11–23.

Morrison, G. R., Ross, S. M., & Kemp, J. E. (2006). *Designing effective instruction* (5th ed.) John Wiley & Sons, Inc.

Nelson, B., Ketelhut, D. J., Clarke, J., Bowman, C., & Dede, C. (2005). Design-based research strategies for developing a scientific inquiry curriculum in a multi-user virtual environment. *Educational Technology, 45*(1), 21–28.

Nguyen, F. (2005). EPSS needs assessment: Oops, I forgot how to do that! *Performance Improvement, 44*(9), 33–39.

Nguyen, F., Klein, J. D., & Sullivan, H. (2005). A comparative study of electronic performance support systems. *Performance Improvement Quarterly, 18*(4), 71–86.

Nieveen, N., & van den Akker, J. (1999). Exploring the potential of a computer tool for instructional developers. *Educational Technology Research and Development, 47*(3), 77–98.

Norton, T. C. (2004a). Usability. In A. Kovalchick & K. Dawson (Eds.), *Education and technology: An encyclopedia, Volume 2:J-Z* (pp. 579–584) Santa Barbara, CA: ABC-CLIO, Inc.

Norton, T. C. (2004b). Web-based surveys. In A. Kovalchick & K. Dawson (Eds.), *Education and technology: An encyclopedia, Volume 2:J-Z* (pp. 644–650) Santa Barbara, CA: ABC-CLIO, Inc.

Orr, S. K. (2005). New technology and research: An analysis of Internet survey methodology in political science. *PS: Politics & Science, 38*(2), 263–267.

Ottevanger, W. (2001). Teacher support materials as a catalyst for science curriculum implementation in Namibia (Doctoral dissertation, Universiteit Twente [The Netherlands], 2001).

Patten, M. L. (2002). *Proposing empirical research: A guide to the fundamentals* (2nd ed.). Los Angeles: Pyrczak Publishing.

Patten, M. L. (2004). *Understanding research methods: An overview of essentials.* (4th ed.). Glendale: Pyrczak Publishing.

Patton, M. Q. (2001). *Qualitative evaluation and research methods* (3rd ed.). Thousand Oaks, CA: Sage.

Patton, M. Q. (1987). *How to use qualitative methods in evaluation.* Newbury Park, CA: Sage Publications, Inc.

Perez, R. S., & Emery, C. D. (1995). Designer thinking: How novices and experts think about instructional design. *Performance Improvement Quarterly, 8*(3), 80–95.

Phillips, J. H. (2000). Evaluating training programs for organizational impact (Doctoral dissertation, Wayne State University, 2000). *Dissertation Abstracts International-A 61*(03), 840.

Plass, J. L., & Salisbury, M. W. (2002). A living-systems design model for web-based knowledge management systems. *Educational Technology Research and Development, 50*(1), 35–57.

Plummer, K. H., Gillis, P. D., Legree, P. J., & Sanders, M. G. (1992). The development and evaluation of a job aid to support mobile subscriber radio-telephone terminal (MSRT). *Performance Improvement Quarterly, 5*(1), 90–105.

Preese, F., & Foshay, W. (1999). The PLATO courseware development environment. In J. van den Akker, R. M. Branch, K. Gustafson, N. Nieveen & T. Plomp's (Eds.), *Design approaches and tools in education and training* (pp. 195–204). Dordrecht, The Netherlands: Kluwer Academic Publishers.

Quiñones, M. A., Ford, J. K., Sego, D. J., & Smith, E. M. (1995/1996). The effects of individual and transfer environment characteristics on the opportunity to perform trained tasks. *Training Research Journal, 1*(1), 29–49.

Ragan, T. J., & Smith, P. L. (2004). Conditions theory and models for designing instruction. In D. Jonassen (Ed.), *Handbook of research for educational communications and technology* (2nd ed.) (pp. 623–649). Mahwah, NJ: Lawrence Erlbaum Associates, Publishers.

Raybould, G. (1995). Performance support engineering: An emerging development methodology for enabling organizational learning. *Performance Improvement Quarterly, 8*(1), 7–22.

Reeves, T. C. (2005). Design-based research in educational technology: Progress made, challenges remain. *Educational Technology, 45*(1), 48–52.

Reigeluth, C. M. (1983). Instruction design: What is it and why is it? In C. M. Reigeluth (Ed.), *Instructional design theories and models* (pp. 3–36). Mahwah, NJ: Lawrence Erlbaum Associates, Publishers.

Reigeluth, C. M. (Ed.). (1999). *Instructional design theories and models, Volume II: A new paradigm of instructional theory.* Mahwah, NJ: Lawrence Erlbaum Associates, Publishers.

Reigeluth, C. M., & Frick, T. W. (1999). Formative research: A methodology for creating and improving design theories. In C. M. Reigeluth (Ed.), *Instructional design theories and models, Volume II: A new paradigm of instructional theory* (pp. 633–651). Mahwah, NJ: Lawrence Erlbaum Associates, Publishers.

Reiser, R. A. (2002). A history of instructional design and technology. In R. A. Reiser & J. V. Dempsey (Eds.), *Trends and issues in instructional design and technology* (pp. 26–53). Upper Saddle River, NJ: Pearson Prentice Hall.

Reiser, R. A., & Dempsey, J. V. (Eds.). (2007). *Trends and issues in instructional design and technology* (2nd ed.). Upper Saddle River, NJ: Pearson Prentice Hall.

Richey, R. C. (1986). *Theoretical and conceptual bases of instructional design.* London: Kogan Page.

Richey, R. C. (1992). *Designing instruction for the adult learner: Systemic training theory and practice.* London/Bristol, PA: Kogan Page/Taylor and Francis.

Richey, R. C. (1997). Agenda-building and its implications for theory construction in instructional technology. *Educational Technology, 37*(1), 5–11.

Richey, R. C. (1998). The pursuit of useable knowledge in instructional technology. *Educational Technology Research and Development, 46*(4), 7–22.

Richey, R. C. (2005). Validating instruction design and development models. In J. M. Spector & D. A. Wiley (Eds.), *Innovations in instructional technology: Essays in honor of M. David Merrill* (pp. 171–185). Mahwah, NJ: Lawrence Erlbaum Associates, Publishers.

Richey, R., Fields, D., & Foxon, M. (2001). *Instructional design competencies: The standards* (3rd ed.). Syracuse, NY: ERIC Clearinghouse on Information & Technology.

Richey, R. C., & Klein, J. D. (2005). Developmental research methods: Creating knowledge from instructional design and development practice. *Journal of Computing in Higher Education, 16*(2), 23–38.

Richey, R. C., Klein, J., & Nelson, W. (2004). Developmental research: Studies of instructional design and development. In D. Jonassen (Ed.), *Handbook of research for educational communications and technology* (2nd ed.) (pp. 1099–1130). Mahwah, NJ: Lawrence Erlbaum Associates, Publishers.

Richey, R. C., & Nelson, W. (1996). Developmental Research. In D. Jonassen (Ed.) *Handbook of research for educational communications and technology* (pp. 1213–1245). New York: Simon & Schuster.

Ross, S. M., & Morrison, G. R. (2004). Experimental research methods. In D. Jonassen (Ed.), *Handbook of research for educational communications and technology* (2nd ed.) (pp. 1021–1043). Mahwah, NJ: Lawrence Erlbaum Associates, Publishers.

Rossett, A. (1999). *First things fast: A handbook for performance analysis.* San Francisco: Jossey-Bass/Pfeifer.

Rowland, G. (1992). What do instructional designers actually do? An initial investigation of expert practice. *Performance Improvement Quarterly, 5*(2), 65–86.

Roytek, M. A. (2000). Contextual factors affecting the use of rapid prototyping within the design and development of instruction (Doctoral dissertation, Wayne State University, 1999). *Dissertation Abstracts International-A, 61*(01), 76.

Rudestam, K. E., & Newton, R. R. (2001). *Surviving your dissertation: A comprehensive guide to content and process* (2nd ed.). Thousand Oaks, CA: Sage Publications.

Russell, C. M. (1990). The development and evaluation of an interactive videodisc system to train radiation therapy technology students on the use of the linear accelerator (Doctoral dissertation, University of Pittsburgh, 1988). *Dissertation Abstracts International-B, 50*(3), 919.

Ryan, M., Hodson-Carlton, K., & Ali, N. S. (2005). A model for faculty teaching online: Confirmation of a dimensional matrix. *Journal of Nursing Education, 44*(8), 357–365.

Saroyan, A. (1993). Differences in expert practice: A case from formative evaluation. *Instructional Science, 21*, 451–472.

Seels, B., & Glasgow, Z. (1998). *Making instructional design decisions* (2nd ed.). Columbus, OH: Merrill Publishing Company.

Seels, B. B., & Richey, R. C. (1994). *Instructional technology: The definition and domains of the field.* Washington, DC: Association for Educational Communications and Technology.

Shellnut, B. J. (1999). The influence of designer and contextual variables on the incorporation of motivational components to instructional design and the perceived success of a project (Doctoral dissertation, Wayne State University, 1999). *Dissertation Abstracts International-A, 60*(06), 1993.

Shellnut, B. J., Knowlton, A., & Savage, T. (1999). Applying the ARCS model to the design and development of computer-based modules for manufacturing engineering courses. *Educational Technology Research and Development, 47*(2), 100–110.

Simon, H. A., & Chase, W. G. (1973). Skill in chess. *American Science, 61,* 394–403.

Singleton, R. A., Jr., & Straits, B. C. (2005). *Approaches to social research* (4th ed.). New York: Oxford University Press.

Sleezer, C. M. (1991). The development and validation of a performance analysis for training model. (Vol. I –III)(Doctoral dissertation, University of Minnesota, 1990). *Dissertation Abstracts International- A, 52*(01), 144.

Sloane, F. C., & Gorard, S. (2003). Exploring modeling aspects of design experiments. *Educational Researcher, 32*(1), 29–31.

Smaldino, S. E., Russell, J. D., Heinich, R., & Molenda, M. (2005). *Instructional technology and media for learning* (8th ed.). Upper Saddle River, NJ: Pearson/Merrill Prentice Hall.

Small, R. V., & Gluck, M. (1994). The relationship of motivational conditions to effective instructional attributes: A magnitude scaling approach. *Educational Technology, 34*(8), 33–40.

Smith, P. L., & Ragan, T. J. (2005). *Instructional design* (3rd ed.). Hoboken, NJ: John Wiley & Sons, Inc.

Spector, J. M., Muraida, D. J., & Marlino, M. R. (1992). Cognitively based models of courseware development. *Educational Technology Research and Development, 40*(2), 45–54.

Spector, J. M., & Song, D. (1995). Automated instructional design advising. In R. D. Tennyson & A. E. Baron (Eds.), *Automating instructional design: Computer-based development and delivery tools* (pp. 377–402). Brussels, Belgium: Springer-Verlag.

Stolovitch, H. D., & Keeps, E. J. (Eds.). (1999). *Handbook of human performance technology* (2nd Ed.). San Francisco: Jossey-Bass/Pfeiffer.

Sullivan, H., Ice, K., & Niedermeyer, F. (2000). Long-term instructional development: A 20-year ID and implementation project. *Educational Technology Research and Development, 48*(4), 87–99.

Surry, D. W., & Ely, D. P. (2002). Adoption, diffusion, implementation, and institutionalization of instructional design and technology. In R. A. Reiser & J. V. Dempsey (Eds.), *Trends and issues in instructional design and technology* (pp. 183–193). Upper Saddle River, NJ: Pearson Prentice Hall.

Taylor, B., & Ellis, J. (1991). An evaluation of instructional systems development in the Navy. *Educational Technology Research and Development, 39*(1), 93–103.

Teachout, M. S., Sego, D. J., & Ford, J. K. (1997/1998). An integrated approach to summative evaluation for facilitating training course improvement. *Training Research Journal, 3,* 169–184.

Tessmer, M., McCann, D., & Ludvigsen, M. (1999). Reassessing training programs: A model for identifying training excesses and deficiencies. *Educational Technology Research and Development, 47*(2), 86–99.

Tessmer, M., & Richey, R. C. (1997). The role of context in learning and instructional design. *Educational Technology Research and Development, 45*(2), 85–115.

Tracey, M. W. (2002). The construction and validation of an instructional design model for incorporating multiple intelligences (Doctoral dissertation, Wayne State University, 2001). *Dissertation Abstracts International-A, 62*(12), 4135.

Tracey, M. W., & Richey, R. C. (in press). ID model construction and validation: A multiple intelligences case. *Educational Technology Research & Development.*

Tuckman, B. W. (1999). *Conducting educational research* (5th ed.). Belmont, CA: Wadsworth Group/Thomson Learning.

Twitchell, S., Holton, E. F., & Trott, J. W. (2000). Technical training evaluation practices in the United States. *Performance Improvement Quarterly, 13*(3), 84–110.

van den Akker, J. (1999). Principles and methods of development research. In J. van den Akker, R. M. Branch, K. Gustafson, N. Nieveen & T. Plomp's (Eds.) *Design approaches and tools in education and training* (pp. 1–14). Dordrecht, The Netherlands: Kluwer Academic Publishers.

van Merrienboer, J. J. G., & Dijkstra, S. (1997). The four-component instructional design model for training complex cognitive skills. In R. D. Tennyson, F. Schot, N. M. Seel, & S. Dijkstra (Eds.), *Instructional design: International perspectives, Volume 1: Theory research and models* (pp. 427–445). Mahwah, NJ: Lawrence Erlbaum Associates, Publishers.

Visscher-Voerman, J. I. A. (2000). Design approaches in training and education: A reconstructive study (Doctoral dissertation, Universiteit Twente [The Netherlands], 1999). *Dissertation Abstracts International-C, 61*(03), 638.

Visscher-Voerman, I., & Gustafson, K. L. (2004). Paradigms in the theory and practice of education and training design. *Educational Technology Research and Development, 52*(2), 69–89.

Visser, L. (1998). The development of motivational communication in distance education support. (Doctoral dissertation, University of Twente, NL).

Visser, L., Plomp, T., Amirault, R. J., & Kuiper, W. (2002). Motivating students at a distance: The case of an international audience. *Educational Technology Research and Development, 50*(2), 94–110.

Wallen, N. E., & Fraenkel, J. R. (2001). *Educational research: A guide to the process* (2nd ed.). Mahwah, NJ: Lawrence Erlbaum Associates, Publishers.

Wang, F., & Hannafin, M. J. (2005). Design-based research and technology-enhanced learning environments. *Educational Technology Research and Development, 53*(4), 5–23.

Wang, F. K., Moore, J. L., Wedman, J., & Shyu, C. R. (2003). Developing a case-based reasoning knowledge repository to support a learning community—An example from the technology integration community. *Educational Technology Research and Development, 51*(3), 45–62.

Weston, C., McAlpine, L., & Bordonaro, T. (1995). A model for understanding formative evaluation in instructional design. *Educational Technology Research and Development, 43*(3), 29–48.

Wiley, D. A. (Ed.). (2000). *Instructional use of learning objects.* Bloomington, IN: Association for Educational Communications and Technology.

Willis, J. (1995). A recursive, reflective instructional design model based on constructivist-interpretivist theory. *Educational Technology, 35*(6), 5–23.

Winn, W. (2004). Cognitive perspectives in psychology. In D. Jonassen (Ed.), *Handbook of research for educational communications and technology* (2nd ed.) (pp. 79–112). Mahwah, NJ: Lawrence Erlbaum Associates, Publishers.

Wolfe, P., Wetzel, M., Harris, G., Mazour, T., & Riplinger, J. (1991). *Job task analysis: Guide to good practice.* Englewood Cliffs, NJ: Educational Technology Publications.

Young, A. C., Reiser, R. A., & Dick, W. (1998). Do *superior* teachers employ systematic instructional planning procedures? A descriptive study. *Educational Technology Research and Development, 46*(2), 65–78.

Zielinski, D. (2000). Objects of desire. *Training, 37*(9), 126–134.

Author Index

Adamski, A. J., 95, 141, 161
Albero-Andres, M., 148, 161
Alessi, S. M., 148, 161
Ali, N. S., 128, 169
Alkin, M. C., 166
Allen, B., 9, 165
Amirault, R. J., 41, 48, 171
Armstrong, A., 86, 161
Aukerman, M. E., 148, 161

Baker, E. L., 145, 161
Banathy, B. H., 6, 161
Baron, A. E., 170
Beauchamp, M., 92, 93, 161
Bennett, A., 130, 141, 164
Berg, B. L., 130, 141, 161
Bevill, L., 165
Bichelmeyer, B., 159, 161
Bordonaro, T., 68, 171
Borg, W. R., 16, 25, 88, 164
Bowman, C., 147, 167
Bracht, G. H., 89, 161
Brady, H. E., 155, 156, 157, 161
Bramble, W., 51, 166
Branch, R. C., 2, 11, 79, 163
Breman, J., 74, 94, 162
Brewer, J., 90, 123, 162
Brewer, S., 165
Briggs, L. J., xvi, 158, 162
Brinkerhoff, J., 165
Broderick, M., 22, 162

Brolin, R. M., 12, 62
Brown, A. L., 146, 162

Cady, M., 148, 165
Cambre, M. A., 148, 162
Campbell, D. T., 36, 60, 72, 162
Carey, J. O., 2, 157, 162
Carey, L., 2, 66, 71, 157, 162
Carliner, S., 11, 93, 94, 162
Carr-Chellman, A., 74, 81, 94, 162
Charness, N., 101, 163
Chase, C. A., 81, 162
Chase, W. G., 101, 170
Cherow-O'Leary, R., 52, 91, 166
Chomei, T., 20, 162
Chou, C., 54, 55, 56, 63, 162
Clark, R. E., 3, 162
Clarke, J., 147, 167
Cobb, R. W., 18, 162
Cochran, W., 94, 162
Collier, D., 155, 156, 157, 161
Collins, A., 146, 162
Corno, L., 150, 162
Corry, M. D., 22, 42, 48, 49, 50, 63, 162
Cowell, D. M., 43, 68, 96, 113, 137, 163
Creswell, J. W., 159, 163
Cunningham, D. J., 5, 163
Cuyar, C., 74, 94, 162

Davidsen, P. I., 19, 167
Davies, I. K., 3, 163

Dawson, K., 161, 167
Dede, C., 147, 167
de la Teja, I., 94, 165
Dempsey, J. V., 27, 165, 168, 170
Design-Based Research Collective, 146, 147, 156, 163
Dessinger, J. C., 155, 163
Dick, W., xix, 2, 22, 66, 71, 150, 157, 163, 172
Dijkstra, S., 23, 151, 163, 171
Donovan, T., 30, 38, 130, 160, 165
Drake, L., 22, 167
Driscoll, M. P., 9, 151, 163, 164
Duffy, T. M., 5, 163
Dwyer, F. M., 12, 166

Edmonds, G. S., 79, 163
Elder, C. D., 18, 162, 164
Ellis, J., 70, 71, 80, 170
Ely, D., 151, 163, 170
Emery, C. D., 80, 102, 131, 167
Ericsson, K. A., 101, 102, 163
Estes, F., 3, 162

Fields, D., 94, 110, 169
Finn, J. D., 2, 163
Fischer, K. M., 10, 52, 53, 63, 163
Flanagan, J. C., 156, 163
Ford, J. K., 52, 53, 69, 168, 170
Forsyth, J. E., 11, 62, 68, 80, 164
Foshay, W., 10, 168
Fowler, F. J., 110, 164
Fox, E. J., 93, 164
Foxon, M., 94, 164, 169
Fraenkel, J. R., 30, 155, 157, 158, 160, 171
Frankfort-Nachmias, C., 36, 37, 158, 159, 164
Freeman, P., 24, 164
Frick, T. W., 22, 42, 48, 49, 50, 147, 148, 157, 162, 168

Gage, N. L., 162
Gagne, R. M., 5, 23, 92, 164
Gall, J. P., 16, 25, 164
Gall, M. D., 16, 25, 164
Gardner, H., 24, 151, 164
Gay, G., 41, 164
George, A. L., 130, 141, 164
Gettman, D., 54, 92, 164

Gilbert, N. J., 151, 164
Gillis, P. D., 42, 168
Glasgow, Z., 2, 169
Glass, G. V., 89, 161
Gluck, M., 12, 170
Golas, K. C., 23, 164
Gorard, S., 147, 170
Grabowski, B., 94, 165
Greenhill, L. P., 20, 164
Gustafson, K., 2, 11, 73, 79, 80, 148, 164, 168, 171

Hallamon, T. C., 74, 81, 164
Hannafin, M. J., 147, 149, 171
Hansen, L., 22, 42, 48, 49, 50, 162
Harris, G., 160, 172
Harris, M., 148, 165
Heinich, R., xvi, 2, 165, 170
Higgins, N., 72, 165
Hilgard, E. R., 145, 165
Hirumi, A., 9, 165
Hoban, C. F., 20, 165
Hodson-Carlton, K., 128, 169
Holton, E. F., 43, 93, 171
Hoover, K. R., 30, 38, 130, 160, 165
Houlihan, R., 20, 162
Hunter, A., 90, 123, 162

Ice, K., 19, 51, 170
ID2 Research Group, 22, 167

Johnson, R. B., 42, 165
Jonassen, D., 12, 26, 163, 165, 166, 168, 169, 171
Jones, T. S., 18, 19, 66, 79, 80, 81, 89, 96, 109, 137, 159, 165

Kaner, J. H., 20, 165
Keeps, E. J., 26, 170
Keller, J. M., 12, 23, 164, 165
Kemp, J. E., 2, 159, 167
Keohand, R. O., 37, 165
Ketelhut, D. J., 147, 167
King, G., 37, 155, 165
Klein, J. D., xv, 1, 9, 10, 20, 26, 28, 87, 93, 94, 134, 164, 165, 167, 169
Knowlton, A., 48, 170

Koroghlanian, C., 165
Koszalka, T. A., 92, 166
Kovalchick, A., 161
Kramlinger, T., 163
Krejcie, R. V., 92, 166
Ku, H., 165
Kuiper, W., 41, 48, 171

Lacy, M. J., 22, 167
Lange, P. C., 166
Leedy, P. D., 89, 166
Legree, P. J., 42, 168
Le Maistre, C., 72, 73, 166
Levine, H. G., 114, 166
Ley, K., xix
Li, Z., 10, 166
Link, N., 52, 91, 166
Littlejohn, S. W., 130, 166
Ludvigsen, M., 24, 66, 170
Luiz, T., 41, 166
Lumsdaine, A. A., 20, 166

MacPherson-Coy, A., 165
Markle, S. M., 2, 166
Marlino, M. R., 11, 12, 66, 67, 137, 170
Martin, B., 51, 166
Mauraida, D., 11, 54, 66, 67, 92, 137, 164, 170
Mazour, T., 160, 172
Mazur, J., 41, 164
McAlpine, L., 68, 171
McCann, D., 24, 66, 170
McCracken, G., 113, 166
McKenney, S., xix, 43, 62, 106, 108, 110, 111, 166
McLellan, H., 20, 166
McNelly, T., 54, 92, 164
Milheim, W. D., 12, 162
Mooij, T., 63, 167
Morrison, G. R., 2, 41, 159, 167, 169
Moseley, J. L., 155, 163
Mukherjee, P., 79, 163
Means, T. B., 12, 166
Medley, D. M., 114, 115, 166
Merrill, M. D., 10, 22, 70, 166, 167
Milrad, M., 19, 167
Molenda, M., xvi, 170

Moore, J. L., 131, 171
Morgan, D. W., 92, 166

Nachmias, D., 36, 37, 158, 159, 164
Nelson, B., 147, 167
Nelson, W., xv, 1, 9, 20, 169
Newton, R. R., 89, 90, 159, 169
Nguyen, F., 10, 134, 165, 167
Niedermeyer, F., 19, 51, 170
Nieveen, N., 10, 54, 56, 63, 164, 167, 168, 171
Norton, T. C., 160, 167

Onwuegbuzie, A. J., 42, 165
Orr, S. K., 118, 119, 167
O'Shea, T., 162
Ottevanger, W., 91, 114, 115, 116, 167

Patten, M. L., 15, 26, 30, 90, 167
Patton, M. Q., 38, 89, 167
Perez, R. S., 25, 80, 102, 131, 167
Phillips, J. H., 80, 167
Plass, J. L., 11, 137, 168
Plomp, T., 41, 48, 171
Plummer, K. H., 42, 168
Pratt, J. A., 22, 167
Preese, F., 10, 168

Quinones, M. A., 69, 80, 168

Ragan, T. J., 2, 6, 168, 170
Randi, J., 150, 162
Raybould, G., 149, 168
Reeves, T. C., 146, 148, 164, 168
Reigeluth, C. M., 5, 26, 147, 148, 157, 162, 166, 168
Reiser, R., xvi, 20, 27, 165, 168, 170, 172
Reisslein, J., 165
Richey, R. C., xv, xvi, 1, 2, 5, 9, 12, 16, 17, 18, 19, 20, 23, 28, 66, 67, 68, 79, 81, 89, 94, 103, 109, 110, 137, 155, 156, 157, 158, 159, 164, 165, 168, 169, 170, 171
Riplinger, J., 160, 172
Roberts, R., 94, 164
Robson, R., 167
Rosenstein, A. J., 20, 165
Ross, S. M., 2, 41, 159, 167, 169

Rudestam, K. E., 89, 90, 159, 169
Rushby, N., 26, 28, 165
Rossett, A., 119, 169
Rowland, G., 80, 102, 131, 169
Roytek, M. A., 12, 79, 169
Russell, C. M., 48, 169
Russell, J. D., xvi, 170
Ryan, M., 128, 169

Salisbury, M. W., 11, 137, 168
Sanders, M. G., 42, 168
Saroyan, A., 89, 169
Savage, T., 48, 170
Savenye, W. C., 9, 10, 52, 163, 165
Scanlon, E., 162
Schott, F., 163
Seel, N. M., 163
Seels, B., xv, xvi, xix, 1, 2, 155, 156, 157, 158, 159, 169
Sego, D. J., 52, 53, 69, 168, 170
Shellnut, B. J., 48, 81, 169, 170
Shyu, C. R., 131, 171
Simon, H. A., 101, 170
Singleton, R. A., Jr., 43, 61, 155, 156, 170
Sleezer, C. M., 12, 170
Sloane, F. C., 147, 170
Smaldino, S. E., xvi, 170
Small, R. V., 12, 170
Smith, E. M., 69, 168
Smith, P. L., 2, 6, 168, 170
Song, D., 148, 170
Spannaus, T., 94, 164
Spector, J. M., 11, 12, 19, 66, 67, 94, 137, 148, 165, 167, 169, 170
Stanley, J. C., 36, 60, 72, 162
Stolovitch, H. D., 26, 170
Straits, B. C., 43, 61, 155, 156, 170
Sullivan, H. J., 10, 19, 51, 52, 63, 89, 134, 163, 167, 170

Sun C., 54, 55, 56, 63, 162
Surry, D. W., 151, 170

Taylor, B., 70, 71, 80, 170
Teachout, M. S., 52, 53, 54, 170
Tennyson, R. D., 163
Tessmer, M., 24, 66, 103, 170
Tracey, M. W., xix, 24, 42, 68, 71, 151, 170, 171
Travers, R. M. W., 161
Trott, J. W., 43, 93, 171
Tuckman, B. W., 16, 25, 171
Twitchell, S., 43, 93, 171

van den Akker, J., 1, 9, 10, 62, 164, 166, 167, 168, 171
van Merrienboer, J. J. G., 23, 151, 171
Verba, S., 37, 165
Viechnicki, K. J., 12, 162
Visscher-Voerman, I., 3, 72, 73, 79, 80, 171
Visser, L., 41, 48, 49, 62, 171

Wager, W. W., 23, 164
Wallen, N. E., 30, 155, 157, 158, 160, 171
Wang, F., 147, 149, 171
Wang, F. K., 131, 171
Wedman, J., 131, 171
Weston, C., 68, 171
Wetzel, M., 160, 172
Wiley, D. A., 21, 171
Willis, J., 151, 171
Winn, W., xix, 146, 171
Winter, C., 165
Wolfe, P., 160, 172

Young, A. C., 150, 172

Zemke, R., 163
Zielinski, D., 21, 172

Subject Index

Automated design tools, 10

Causal inference, 37, 58, 76, 130, 155
Constructivism, 5, 139, 151
  Definition of, 155
Context, see also setting
  Data, 102, 104, 128, 139
  Effects of, 12, 63, 75, 84, 103, 139, 141
  Organizational climate, 63, 79, 80, 84, 103
Critical incident technique, 113, 115
  Definition of, 156

Data collection, instrumentation
  Examples of, 108, 109, 110, 111, 112, 114,
    115, 116, 117
  Interview protocols, 113
  Observation guides, 113
  Surveys, 110
  Web-based surveys, 118
  Work logs, 103, 106, 109
Data collection, issues
  Model research, 78
  Organizational restrictions, 124
  Product and tool research, 61
  Response rate, 119
  Self-reports, 53, 123, 137
  Web-based data collection, 118
Data collection, technology-based
  Laboratory-based, 120

Software-based, 120, 121
Web-based, 118
Data, types of
  Context data, 102, 104, 155
  Extant data, 66, 76, 79, 111, 123, 157
  In-progress data, 103, 105, 133, 137
  Profile data, 100, 110, 139, 159
  Retrospective data, 19, 31, 78, 103, 109,
    123, 136, 140, 159
  Try-out data, 58, 106, 107, 147, 160
Descriptive research
  Definition of, 43, 156
  Examples of, 45, 48, 52, 56, 57, 68, 72,
    134, 136
Design and development research
  Contributions of, 127
  Definition of, xv, 1, 156
  Expansion of, 146, 151
  Laboratory for, 120
  Methodology, 40, 44
  Need for, 2
  Outcomes of, 13
  Parameters of, 31
  Process checklists, 33, 46, 64, 82, 97,
    126, 143
  Publication of, 27
  Role of, 14
  Scope, 7
  Types of, 8, 9, 10

Design and development
  Advancement of, 6
  Knowledge base, 3, 7, 15, 128, 152
  Science of, 2, 22
  Theory construction, 129, 150
  Theory of, 6, 22, 130
Design-based research, 146
  Definition of, 156
Design cycle time, 6, 104
  Definition of, 156
Designer research
  Designer characteristics, 12, 24, 81, 110
  Designer expertise, 12, 24, 25, 30, 67, 72,
    80, 92, 100, 131, 139
  Designer thinking & decision-making, 12,
    22, 24, 73, 93
Developmental research, xv, 1
Distance education, 20, 26, 27
  Research on, 48, 55, 92, 128

Electronic performance support systems
    (EPSS), 149
  Research on, 10, 92, 134
Ethical issues, 16, 94, 96
Evaluation
  Confirmative evaluation, 12, 32, 155
  Course evaluation, 70
  Formative evaluation, 9, 10, 21, 32, 52, 55,
    56, 68, 72, 92, 104, 120, 131, 157
  Product evaluation, 40, 48, 91, 106, 111
  Program evaluation, 51
  Research on, 53, 68, 72, 93
  Summative evaluation, 9, 12, 32, 53,
    104, 159
Explanatory research, 43
  Definition of, 43, 157
  Examples of, 43, 49, 52, 56, 71, 131, 134
Exploratory research
  Definition of, 43, 45, 157
  Examples of, 45, 49, 50, 52, 54, 56, 70, 72,
    73, 74, 131, 136

Formative research, 9, 147
  Definition of, 157

General systems theory, see theory, systems
  theory

Generalizing findings, 131, 141
  Definition of, 157
  Model findings, 77
  Product and tool findings, 59
  Research design and, 38
  Use of case study, 130
  Use of multiple project data, 141
  Use of project-specific data, 140

Informed consent, 95
  Definition of, 157
Instructional design
  Definition of, xvi, 24
  Knowledge base, 3
  Models of, 1, 6, 22, 23, 66, 74, 136,
    139, 151
  Paradigms, 3, 74
  Practice of, 6
Instructional development, xvi
  Definition of, 156
Instructional systems design (ISD),
    see instructional design

Learning objects, 6, 21

Message design, 5
Mixed methods research
  Definition of, 41, 158
  Examples of, 42, 48, 52, 55, 67
Model development research
  Conclusions of, 135
  Definition of, 11
  Design of, 137
  Examples of, 66, 67, 137
Model research
  Conclusions of, 13, 135
  Definition of, 10, 158
  Design Issues, 78
  Design of, 75
  Interpreting findings, 135
  Methods of, 65, 137
  Parameters of, 32
  Types of, 8, 10, 76
Model use research
  Conclusions of, 138, 140
  Definition of, 12
  Examples of, 72, 73, 74

Model validation research
  Conclusions of, 26, 137
  Definition of, 11
  Examples of, 68, 69, 70, 71, 92
  External validation, 23, 24, 70, 137, 157
  Internal validation, 12, 23, 68, 137, 158
Multiple methods research
  Definition of, 41, 158
  Examples of, 49, 53, 66, 74

Needs assessment
  Definition of, 158
  Research on, 9, 10, 24, 43, 113
Non-instructional intervention, 9, 10, 134,
  141, 149

Online learning, see distance education
Outcomes, see conclusions of

Participants
  Characteristics of, 80, 100, 133, 135
  Examples of, 91
  Impact of, 130, 134, 139, 140
  Protection of, 94, 142
  Recruitment of, 118
  Selection of, 37, 87, 90
  Types of, 80, 87
Performance improvement, xvi, 18, 93, 149
  Definition of, 159
Product and tool research
  Conclusions of, 13, 132, 135
  Definition of, 9, 159
  Design issues, 61
  Design of, 57
  Examples of, 9, 10, 48, 49, 51, 52, 53, 55,
    56, 91
  Interpreting findings, 132
  Methods of, 47
  Parameters of, 31
  Types of, 8, 9, 58

Qualitative research
  Causality in, 37
  Data triangulation, 123, 160
  Definition of, 159
  Examples of, 49, 66, 70, 73, 74, 131
  Generalization issues, 130, 131, 140

  Methods of, 38, 113, 114
  Nature of, 42
  Sampling in, 90
  Validity of, 37
Quantitative research
  Causality in, 37
  Definition of, 159
  Examples of, 53, 70, 71, 134
  Methods of, 114
  Nature of, 42
  Sampling in, 89
  Validity of, 36, 38, 89

Rapid prototyping
  Definition of, 159
  Research on, 12, 66, 75
Recall data, see data, retrospective data
Research literature
  Conference proceedings, 28
  Dissertations, 27, 48
  Journals, 26, 48
  Workplace documents, 28
Research design, 36, 38
  Components of, 39
  Definition of, 159
Research methods
  Types of, 44, 56, 134
Research questions
  Answering, 28, 85, 133
  Data collection and, 100
  Data sets and, 100, 124
  Expansion of, 73, 131
  Research methodology and, 39, 41, 42
  Research problems and, 29
  Sampling and, 90
  Writing, 29
Research problems
  Emerging, 131
  Focusing, 29, 33
  Identifying, 15, 24, 25, 28, 33
  Sources of, 16, 23

Sampling
  Convenience samples, 90
  Issues, 90, 118, 124
  Random sampling, 38, 89, 90, 92,
    93, 159

Sampling (*continued*)
  Purposeful sampling, 38, 89, 90, 91, 93,
    94, 159
  Stratified, 94
  Theory and, 130
Setting, see also context
  Examples of, 74, 91, 134
  Impact of, 78, 79, 91, 103, 129, 131
  Interpretation and, 128
  Issues, 62, 86, 149
  Research design and, 32, 37, 38, 115
  Research findings and, 60, 69, 85
  Research questions and, 85
  Research problems and, 17
  Sampling and, 89
  Selection of, 85, 89
  Types of, 11, 74, 84, 90, 119

Teaching-learning research, 5, 6, 87, 146
Technology research
  Examples of, 49, 55, 56, 67, 93, 147, 149
  Sources of research problems, 19, 148
Theory
  Definition of, 160
  Communication theory, 5, 22
  Instructional theory, 5, 22
  Learning Theory, 4, 6, 148, 22
  Systems theory, 6, 22

Theory-based research
  Examples of, 24, 150, 151
  Sources of research problems, 22, 150
Think-aloud methods
  Definition of, 160
  Elements of, 80
  Examples of, 50, 72
  Technology for, 121
Transfer of training
  Predictors of, 5, 80, 103
  Research on, 53, 69, 103

Usability
  Research on, 49, 55, 68

Validity
  Conclusions and, 36, 48, 81, 88, 123
  Establishing, 24, 36, 37, 58, 60, 76, 78
  Types of, 12, 89

Workplace research
  Examples of, 18, 52, 66, 68, 69, 71, 74, 92,
    93, 94, 141
  Issues, 62, 79, 86, 124, 141,149
  Sources of research problems, 17, 149